CALLED TO ACCOUNT

CALLED TO ACCOUNT

*The Case for Police Accountability
in England and Wales*

Sarah Spencer

National Council for Civil Liberties

1985

National Council for Civil Liberties
21 Tabard Street, London SE1 4LA

©Sarah Spencer 1985

British Library Cataloguing in Publication Data

Spencer, Sarah
    Called to Account: the case for police accountability in
    England and Wales
    1. Police — Great Britain — complaints against
    I. Title
    II. National Council for Civil Liberties
    363.2'0941   HV8195.A2

ISBN 0-946088-12-8

Printed in Great Britain by the Russell Press, Nottingham

CONTENTS

	Introduction	1
1	The Background to the 1964 Police Act	9
2	The Police and Elected Representatives (1): The Law	31
3	The Police and Elected Representatives (2): Accountability in Practice	42
4	In Defence of the Status Quo	89
5	Proposals for Reform	109
6	Campaigning for Democratic Control of the Police	136

Acknowledgements

NCCL and the author would like to thank those members of police authorities who agreed to be interviewed and provided essential information for this book; those members of NCCL's local groups whose campaigns to make their own police authorities more effective resulted in information and experience on which the author has drawn; and the following people for their constructive comments on all, or sections of, the draft manuscript: Bob Fine, Paul Gordon, Patricia Hewitt, Paddy Hillyard, Tony Jefferson, Ian Martin, Jeremy McBride, Terry Munyard, Phil Scraton and Marie Staunton.

Introduction

It is a fundamental principle of a democratic system of government that people who are elected, or appointed, to exercise power over others should be accountable for their actions. This principle is not observed in the current system of policing in Britain. Police officers are not accountable to our elected representatives for their decisions and the politicians, in turn, are not fulfilling their responsibilities to the public. This is the unavoidable conclusion of an examination of the respective powers of the police and elected representatives in England and Wales and the way in which policing decisions are being made.

This is not to say that the police, and the national and local politicians who hold some responsibility for them, are abusing their powers (although that is part of the story). The 1964 Police Act, which established the current system, was not intended to place the police on the same footing as other public services:

> . . . the relationship between a police authority and its chief constable will . . . differ from that between other council committees and their chief officers. In the latter case the role of the official is to advise the committee and to implement its decisions on matters of policy; but the decisions themselves are the responsibility of the elected body.
>
> *In the case of the police these positions will be reversed.* The role of the police authority will be to advise the chief constable on general matters connected with the policing of the area, *but decisions will be the responsibility of the chief constable alone* [our emphasis].[1]

The result was the creation of a policing system in which the most senior officials — the chief constables, and the Metropolitan Commissioner in London — were given much greater powers than their local government counterparts: the power to 'direct and control' their forces, with only a limited duty to tell the elected representatives afterwards what they had done. If the politicians did not like what they heard, they were, intentionally, given few powers to do anything about it.

Thus, from the start, the system of accountability was intended to be limited, if indeed it can be called 'accountability' at all. Accountability is a form of control. It has been defined, in the context of policing, in the following way:

a person is accountable to another if he is under a duty to answer to that other for his actions, *that duty being attended by the possibility of disciplinary or similar measures if the actions are disapproved of or are irregular* [our emphasis].[2]

If the system demands little accountability from the police, they sometimes give, in practice, even less. In part, this reflects an unwillingness to provide information when asked; in part, the failure of elected representatives at local and national level to ask for it. Nor do the politicians always prove more accountable for their own decisions. Home Secretaries exercise extensive powers over the police on behalf of Parliament, but provide that body with sparse information about their decisions; the work of the Home Office thus remains inscrutable to the public and MPs alike.

Similarly, as we shall see, the chairmen and chairwomen of police authorities are often left to make decisions with their chief constables between infrequent and often ineffectual meetings of the authorities.

The net result of this system is, first, that major (and minor) developments can take place in policing without prior debate or agreement by Parliament or police authorities. Parliament did not decide, for example, that there should be a rapid shift towards 'reactive' policing methods over the last two decades, yet a recent survey of policing developments could cite a long list of changes that confirm that this shift has taken place: an increasing use of computerised command and control systems; an increasing number of elite, highly mobile task forces (such as the special patrol groups); the existence in all but name of a paramilitary 'third force' to deal with strikes, political violence and demonstrations; the distribution of riot equipment and firearms. The authors of the survey in *State Research* concluded that 'the present "debate" between preserving policing by "consent" (epitomised by the Dixon of Dock Green image) or the adoption of "fire-brigade" (or reactive) policing has, in practice, already been resolved'. Nevertheless, their examination of all official police reports over the period during which these developments have taken place 'shows an almost complete failure to include information on the most contentious developments ... there was virtually no information published at the time, and therefore no basis for scrutiny or public debate by the statutory bodies'.[3]

It is not that these developments are uncontroversial, even within the police force itself. John Alderson, then Chief Constable of Devon and Cornwall, expressed his concern that

most serving police officers in this new age have become

technological 'cops' who barely meet their public outside conflict or crisis . . . loss of human contact, knowledge and understanding, the very essence of democratic policing, is too high a price to pay for technology. The gulf that can arise from these conditions can open up as police drift further into their own reactive style — a gulf which can lead to misunderstanding, suspicions, even to hostility.[4]

A second consequence of the lack of democratic accountability is that the police may not be called to account when their policies, or particular policing incidents, give cause for concern: for example, the low crime clear-up rate; the treatment of suspects in custody; the policing of demonstrations and industrial disputes; the handling of racist attacks; the use of task forces like the special patrol groups; saturation policing methods, and the use of stop-and-search powers; the use of police computers; the surveillance of political and trade union activists; the use of 'supergrasses'; raids to detect illegal immigrants; the policing of gay pubs and clubs. While the civil disturbances in the summer of 1981 focused press and public attention on the question 'Who controls the police?' no issue highlighted the lack of accountability more than the policing of the miners' dispute in 1984-5.

Concern about such issues is not new and goes beyond the question of police abuse of their powers. It is concern about police policies and practices and it cannot be channelled through the usual political machinery to bring about change because the police are not accountable to our elected representatives. The problem is most acute in London because London's locally elected representatives have no responsibility for the police at all, the Home Secretary alone being the police authority for the Metropolitan Police.

This lack of accountability to the public has, we believe, been one major factor in the deteriorating relationship between the police and sections of the community. It is, in part, because of their lack of accountability that the police can remain distant from the public and insensitive to their needs. As Lord Scarman noted (although he did not, in our view, subsequently recommend an adequate solution):

> The opportunity to ignore local opinion (but not national) exists for the Metropolitan Police; and he would be a bold man (bolder than I) who would affirm that the existence of an opportunity does not breed the temptation to make use of it, especially when it is convenient or saves trouble.[5]

His observation applies equally to the rest of the country, despite the presence of locally elected representatives on provincial police authorities. The result of this insensitive policing is a reduction in public support for the police — and hence in their effectiveness — and frustration on the part of the public at their inability to bring about any change.

This concern about the lack of effective accountability has been taken up by a few police authorities and, in London, by the Greater London Council and some borough councils, all demanding a greater say in determining the priorities and methods of the police in their areas — in effect, some control over the way in which their ratepayers' money is spent. Their demands are not new. Nor is the confusion which exists over the respective powers of chief constables, the Home Secretary and police authorities, and the conflict which simmers between a minority of police authorities and their chief constables. Neither of the two conflicting but prevalent notions — that elected representatives did control the police through watch committees before the 1964 Police Act, or that demands for such control are unprecedented — are, as we shall show, supported by the historical record.

One of the government's responses to the growing demands for greater accountability has been to offer the public 'consultation' with the police instead; initially, in June 1982, by issuing a circular encouraging the establishment of (non-elected) liaison (or consultative) committees between the police and 'community leaders'; more recently with a weaker statutory proposal in its Police and Criminal Evidence Act.

Consultation is not, of course, the same as accountability. Even if the police participate in liaison committees (and the new Act does not oblige them to do so), they are not accountable to the committee because they do not have to give them any information at all or take the committee's view into account. Nor can a liaison committee reprimand the police if it disapproves of their actions. Nevertheless, even this limited proposal did not meet with the approval of the Chief Constable of Greater Manchester, James Anderton, who dismissed it scornfully: 'And now the magic word "consultation" has been offered as a panacea to all our plagues. What a wistful delusion that it'.[6]

While James Anderton's senior colleagues probably do not share his hostility to formal consultation arrangements, they are united in rejecting demands that they be made more accountable to elected representatives for their actions. They argue that they are already democratically accountable in that they are accountable to the law (through the courts), and laws are enacted by Parliament. But they insist that their direct accountability to elected representatives cannot be strengthened because of the danger that the politicians would interfere in the impartial enforcement of the law. The police believe that their accountability to the law, and their judgement as professionals, ensure that they enforce the law impartially, and they maintain that this impartiality would be impaired if they lost their independence. Sir Robert Mark, former Commissioner of the Metropolitan Police, actually regarded the danger of democratic control over policing as a more serious threat than terrorism:

> These, then, are the two great problems for the next generation of policemen. Resistance to political encroachment on their operational freedom, and exposure to the brunt of social change. By comparison with those two, crime is never likely to be more than the conventional costly nuisance it is today and terrorism, as today, in reality a comparatively insignificant issue.[7]

This book argues that democratic control over policing is not the threat to the police, or to the public, which Sir Robert Mark believed. Rather, it is both desirable and essential if the police are to carry out their tasks in the interests of the communities they serve. There are many questions which it seeks to answer. How did it come about that the provincial police, in 1964, were made accountable (in theory if not in practice) to a local government committee, one third of the members of which were non-elected magistrates, while in London the police authority was to remain the Home Secretary alone (chapter 1)? What are the respective powers and responsibilities of the members of the 'tripartite structure' — police authorities, the Home Secretary and the police, and how accountable are they all in practice (chapters 2 and 3)? How valid are the arguments put up to defend the status quo: is it true, for instance, that the police must remain free from direction by elected representatives in order to protect their impartiality (chapter 4)? In chapter 4 we also examine minor changes proposed by people who seek to retain the present system of accountability, such as encouraging police authorities to use their existing powers more fully, and establishing a network of consultative committees. We then consider two early proposals which did challenge the structure of accountability — those from Jack Straw MP and from the Association of Metropolitan Authorities (chapter 5).

If it is agreed that the degree of direction from, and accountability to, elected representatives should be enhanced the key questions become: How much control? In what ways should the police be accountable? If the powers of police authorities are to be enhanced, what about the role of parliament? How would the proposed new systems work in practice? What safeguards should be built into the system to guard against corruption? These difficult questions are addressed in chapter 5. Finally, in chapter 6, we look briefly at some of the steps which are being, and could be, taken to further the police accountability campaign.

In formulating proposals for a new institutional structure for accountability the government has, in the case of the metropolitan counties, presented us with a difficulty: the proposed abolition of the metropolitan councils and hence their police authorities, and of the GLC, removes the local government tier covering the same geographical area as the police forces, to which the police could be made accountable.[8] The replacement of the authorities with nominated joint boards would take the police one step further away from democratic accountability. While it remains unclear what form local government will take we restrict our proposals for these areas to the principles on which the structure of accountability should be based.

Changing the law to bring the police under democratic control will not in itself be enough. The absence of accountability is evident in many different aspects of policing, and they do not all require the same solution. There is widespread concern, for example, about the treatment of suspects in police stations, in particular about the pressure put on suspects to make confessions and the admissibility of these confessions at their subsequent trial. The reforms contained in the Police and Criminal Evidence Act will not rectify this situation. Nor have the changes in the police complaints system introduced the effective independent system which is essential to ensure that complaints against the police are investigated vigorously and fairly, so that officers are held accountable if they break the law or violate the Police Discipline Code. The case for reform of the complaints system has already been argued in NCCL's publication *A Fair Cop*.[9]

Nor will democratic control over the police remove the injustice and resentment caused by bad laws: it would not have removed the offence of 'Sus', which had to be removed by Act of Parliament, and it cannot prevent the police enforcing other unpopular laws as long as they remain on the statute book (although it can influence the priority they are given in law enforcement). The solution to bad laws is for Parliament to repeal them.

Data protection legislation with enforceable regulations covering police records is a necessary step to remove the abuse of civil liberties inherent in a system of secret computers and manual records storing personal and political, and often inaccurate, information about millions of individuals. A Freedom of Information Act would ensure that information about policing developments was more easily accessible both to elected representatives and to the public. Over and above these changes in the law, reforms are evidently required in police training and supervision and in the Discipline Regulations. These are only the beginning, and all are beyond the remit of this book.

An effective police complaints system and the introduction of enforceable safeguards for suspects are necessary to ensure that, in exercising their discretion, the police stay within the law and the terms of their Discipline Code. Democratic control over policing has a separate function: to ensure that, in exercising their discretion, both at the level of policy and on the street, the police reflect the needs and priorities of the communities they serve. It is only when they are genuinely accountable to the public that they will do this for, as Lord Scarman recognised:

> Accountability . . . renders the police answerable for what they do. Thereby it prevents them from slipping into an enclosed fortress of inward thinking and social isolation which would in the long term result in a siege mentality — the police in their fortress (happy as long as it is secure) and the rest of us outside, unhappy, uncertain and insecure (for we do not know what they will do, or how they will do it).[10]

It is to help avoid a further deterioration in that direction that this book has been written. It does not seek to provide definitive answers in a debate which is only just beginning. The arguments it puts forward challenge many shibboleths about the independence of the police which even those who are most concerned about current trends in policing rarely presume to question. It is our hope that this book will provide a stimulus to the debate about some of the most difficult questions to be resolved in this crucial area of public policy.

This book covers directly only the position of the regular police forces in England and Wales. The laws governing the relationship between elected representatives and the police in Scotland and Northern Ireland are different from those in England and Wales, as is the nature of that relationship and the problems which arise from it. While the principles of democratic accountability on which the recommendations in this book are based should be equally applicable outside England and Wales (and to the specialised forces such as the Ministry of Defence police and railway police) the specific institutional arrangements through which accountability could be increased may not be.

In a wider context, we recognise that in making the police accountable to elected representatives those politicians remain in many ways unrepresentative of the public. While we do consider in chapter 5 the question of cooption of community representatives on to the police authority, of necessity we take the existing system of local government as given, as the existing form of local democracy in this country. The reforms needed to strengthen that system of democracy are beyond the scope of this book.

Notes
1. *Report of the Royal Commission on the Police* (1962), Cmnd 1728, para.166.
2. Richard Card, 'Police Accountability and Control Over the Police', *Bramshill Journal*, Vol.1, No.1 (Autumn 1979).
3. *State Research Bulletin* 19 (August/September 1980).
4. John Alderson, *Policing Freedom* (1979), pp.41-2.
5. Lord Scarman, *Report on the Disturbances in Brixton 10th to 13th April 1981*, Cmnd 8427, para.5.67.
6. *Police* (April 1982).
7. Robert Mark, *In the Office of Constable* (Fontana, 1979), p.308.
8. 'Streamlining the Cities, Government Proposals for Reorganising Local Government in Greater London and the Metropolitan Counties' (October 1983), White Paper, Cmnd 9063.
9. Patricia Hewitt, *A Fair Cop: Reforming the Police Complaints Procedure* (NCCL, 1982).
10. Scarman Report, *op.cit.*, para.5.58.

CHAPTER 1
The Background to the 1964 Police Act

The current relationship between the police and elected representatives has existed only since the enactment of the 1964 Police Act. This Act was inspired by the findings of the Royal Commission on the Police, which examined the arrangements for controlling the police which had developed, piecemeal, over past centuries and the problems to which they had given rise.

The early history of the police, which we can of necessity cover only in outline, may be divided, simply, into three periods: that prior to the nineteenth century, when a handful of parish constables and justices of the peace shared responsibility for 'keeping the King's Peace'; the years between 1829 and the turn of the century, which saw the gradual development of the 'new police', organised for the first time into local forces under a varying degree of direction from chief constables, justices, elected councillors and the Home Secretary; and the years after 1900 during which the forces amalgamated, new policing techniques and technology improved efficiency, and control of the police became increasingly concentrated in the hands of the Home Office and chief constables.

This early history is marked by four characteristics relevant to an understanding of the police today:

- The piecemeal development of local forces with differing administrative structures in London, the municipal boroughs (towns), and the (rural) counties, each with differing statutory relationships between the police, justices, councillors, and the Home Secretary.
- Continuing and unresolved ambiguity in the common and statutory law over the extent of control to be exercised by the various bodies with responsibility for the police, and the conflicts to which this ambiguity gave rise. No clear trend towards, or away from, accountability to elected representatives emerges.

- The impetus for establishing a network of police forces, and, less successfully, for central control of those forces, came repeatedly from Home Secretaries, often pressing for reforms in face of stiff local and parliamentary opposition.
- The immediate pressure for the successive reforms was not only crime but the continuing threat and reality of public disorder.

The First Constables

Policing has always been a local responsibility in Britain. In the Middle Ages, it was a shared responsibility, everyone (within certain social strata) having a duty to raise 'hue and cry' to catch criminals and to keep arms for that purpose. Unpaid part-time constables were elected in rotation to ensure that this responsibility was carried out, and constables' common law powers and duties stem from this early role. In towns, they had the assistance of paid night watchmen.

In the fourteenth century, justices of the peace were appointed by the Crown with a special responsibility to keep the peace, as well as, in many cases, to preside over the local courts. The arrival of justices reduced the status of the constables, who were their social inferiors and were obliged, under the common law, to carry out the justices' instructions.

Over the years, both constables and justices fell increasingly into disrepute. Although the office of constable was supposed to rotate, those who could afford to pay someone else to take their turn did so, so that by the end of the eighteenth century many of the men who served as parish constables 'were at best illiterate fools, and at worst as corrupt as the criminal classes from which not a few sprang'.[1]

Meanwhile, the justices, who were paid in proportion to the number of persons they convicted, were frequently known to be corrupt and consequently commanded little respect. Yet this was the time of the industrial revolution when the population was both increasing dramatically and moving from rural areas into the cities; a time of great social upheaval and conflict, when crime increased and public disorder became more frequent. We cannot discuss here the nature of this conflict, nor the social causes of the increase in crime and disorder. The result was that the constables and justices were quite unable to cope.

Outside London, some of the towns raised a levy to patch up the old police system by appointing paid constables, but many areas, less affected by social change, retained elected constables. There was, in the eighteenth and early nineteenth centuries, no unified system of local government which could have taken on the responsibility of appointing and administering a police 'force'.

A New Police Force for London

Proposals from the chief magistrates and successive Home Secretaries for an organised police force in London, under a unified command, initially met strong and consistent opposition from a majority in Parliament and in the press. The view of these critics was that an organised police force, far from being a precondition for freedom, as the reformers claimed, would actually be a threat to freedom.

No less than three parliamentary committees, in 1816, 1818 and 1822, rejected the idea of a police force as incompatible with British liberty. The committee that reported in 1822 told the Home Secretary, Robert Peel:

> It is difficult to reconcile an effective system of police, with that perfect freedom of action and exemption from interference, which are the great privileges and blessings of society in this country, and Your Committee think that the forfeiture or curtailment of such advantages would be too great a sacrifice for improvements in police, or facilities in detection of crime, however desirable in themselves if abstractly considered.[2]

This opposition was finally overcome with the enactment of Peel's Metropolitan Police Act of 1829, which created a unified force for the whole of London, excluding the City.

London had for some years been experiencing periodic outbursts of rioting which, coupled with poor economic conditions, unemployment and strikes, 'aroused the fears of the middle class, the manufacturers and the upper classes'.[3] During the debates on Peel's Bill,

> there were outbursts of rioting and framebreaking. *The Times* daily carried reports of violence . . . the trend of events seemed to indicate approaching crisis. The Monarchy was unpopular, republican sentiment was being heard openly, there was fear of revolution, fear of mob, and apprehension for the security of property. The demand for protection became widespread as business and industrial interests exerted pressure which transcended party lines, a pressure which Parliament dare not ignore. The Metropolitan Police Act was passed.[4]

Two justices, later known as 'commissioners', were appointed to direct and control the new police force; they came under the authority of the Home Secretary, and the regulations they devised were subject to his approval. There was no local government structure which could have exercised such control over the force at that time. According to a later Home Secretary (in 1888):

> It was quite plain that it was the intention of the legislature to put the police force under the authority of the Secretary of State and to hold him fully responsible, not for every detail of the management of the force, but in regard to the general policy of the police in the discharge of their duty.[5]

Because of the Home Secretary's direct responsibility for the Metropolitan Police, Members of Parliament were able to question him in the House of Commons. They frequently asked him not only about general policies but also about specific incidents, a right restricted in later years by successive Home Secretaries.

A receiver was appointed to levy a police rate from Londoners to pay for the new force and to manage its property, which included the office of the first two commissioners, Rowan and Mayne, at Scotland Yard. The force was divided (as now) into districts, then each under a superintendent, with inspectors, sergeants and constables in his charge.

The City of London police were excluded solely because of the opposition of the powerful mayor and aldermen, who were reluctant to have their powers reduced. Agreeing to exclude the City ensured Peel an easier passage for his Bill. When threatened by a Bill to amalgamate the two London forces in 1838, the City of London Corporation addressed a petition resisting the move to Queen Victoria, and quickly established an organised force of its own under the control of a commissioner appointed by the corporation.[6]

Critchley, regarded as the most authoritative historian of the police, notes that many Londoners regarded the new London force with 'hostility or derision', parish meetings throughout the city describing it as 'an outrage and insult' to the people; complaints against the police 'poured into Scotland Yard'. He also records that the police were soon in action, dealing with the 'Reform Bill Riot' and 'the growth of subversive activities which provided endless opportunities for the police to perfect techniques of crowd-control and practise the newly acquired art of baton charges'.[7]

Reform in the Towns

The impetus for reform in the towns and counties came in part, as in London, from the outbreaks of civil disturbance and the inability of the 'old police' to restore order. Its development, however, was greatly influenced by the reform of local government, which occurred in the towns before the counties, and which involved a transfer of power from the landed gentry (from whom justices were usually drawn) to the new industrial middle classes, elected as town councillors to control the new municipal corporations.

The 1835 Municipal Corporation Act *required* the new councils to form a 'watch committee', made up of councillors and the mayor (who had to be a justice). In turn, the watch committee had to:

- Appoint a 'sufficient number of fit men' as constables to preserve the peace, prevent robberies and other crimes, and catch offenders (at the ratepayers' expense).
- Frame regulations to prevent 'neglect or abuse' and to make constables efficient.
- Suspend or dismiss any constable whom they considered negligent or otherwise unfit to be a constable, *a power also held by any two justices*.

Constables had the same duties and responsibilities as their predecessors had had under common law, but they now also had a *statutory* duty to 'obey all such commands' from any justice having jurisdiction in the borough.

Notwithstanding these provisions, the 1835 Act, which governed the relationship between watch committees and borough police forces until 1964, did not state clearly *who* was to control the new forces. Justices could give constables lawful orders, but were not organised as a body which could provide overall control or day-to-day supervision. Watch committees were empowered to make regulations, but whether they could instruct their forces was never clear. Moreover, constables' powers were not delegated either by the justices or by the watch committees but were 'original', derived from the common law. They could, therefore, act independently without any instructions. Critchley says that the police were demonstrably *not* under the control of justices,[8] but that the extent to which watch committees could give orders under this legislation remained unresolved until the Act was repealed in 1964.

Brogden gives us some insight into the relationship between one such watch committee and its head constable in the years immediately after the Act was passed.[9] In Liverpool, during the first eleven years of the 'new police' (1835-47), a subcommittee of 'the watch' met *daily* to supervise police operations. It issued, on average, one order a week for the direct placement of officers. It was only once the parameters of police work had become established that the direction of the force was left to the head constable.

Brogden does record, however, that the head constable refused to obey an order of the mayor to ban a Chartist meeting as early as 1841, and in later years his successors defended their autonomy with increasing success. The extent of head (later chief) constables' autonomy was, as we shall see, the subject of marked conflict between chief constables, watch committees and justices on a number of occasions.

There was no provision in the 1835 Act for any form of control or supervision by the Home Secretary, although watch committees had to submit quarterly reports to him covering the number of constables appointed, arms, equipment, wages and buildings, as well as a copy of all rules made for the regulation and guidance of constables. At this stage there was no provision for the reports to be laid before Parliament.

Reform in the Counties

When the government was legislating for borough police forces in 1835, there was no equivalent local government structure in the rural counties to which it could entrust such a responsibility. Yet it found itself obliged to deploy troops, and Metropolitan Police officers, to back up the rural constables, who were now faced with Chartists demanding better living conditions — a movement believed to have a million supporters. As the disturbances spread during the spring of 1839, the Home Secretary received a letter from the major-general in charge of troops in the North of England: 'My belief is that concession must be made to the people's feelings, or the establishment for the strong rural police hurried on . . . if the police force be not quickly increased we shall require troops from Ireland'.[10] The County Police Bill was introduced in Parliament four days later.

In the absence of county councils (which were not established until 1888), the 1839 Act empowered, but did not require, the quarter sessions of local magistrates (justices) to establish a local force, to determine its size, and to appoint (and dismiss) its chief constable — *powers which they exercised subject to the approval of the Home Secretary*. The Home Secretary was also responsible for making the rules governing each force, copies of which were laid before Parliament.

In contrast to the position in the boroughs, it was the responsibility of the chief constable to appoint the other constables in the force (subject to the approval of two justices), and to dismiss them 'at his pleasure'. Moreover, he 'shall have the general Disposition and Government of all the Constables so to be appointed, subject to such lawful orders as he may receive from the Justices . . . and to the Rules established for the Government of the Force'.[11]

The 1839 Act thus gave chief constables in the counties far greater control over their men than their counterparts in the boroughs, where powers to appoint, discipline, promote and dismiss constables were held by the watch committees. The Act also provided for a degree of direction and supervision by central government that did not apply in the boroughs. Indeed, the government would have preferred the forces to be under even greater control, had it not been for the fierce opposition of 'that bastion of the Tory aristocracy, the County magistrates'.[12]

Opposition to the establishment of a permanent police force clearly remained strong, *The Times* describing the proposed county forces as 'an apparatus which we have no question will be very injurious to public and general liberty and the free expression of opinion'.[13]

The 1839 Act did not *require* the magistrates to set up a force, however, and only half the counties chose to do so. The rest continued, in part because of the cost involved, to rely on unpaid amateur constables. However, even the boroughs, which did have a duty to establish a police force, had proved unwilling to fulfil their responsibility. Many reduced the size of their force when the threat of Chartism subsided, and by 1853 thirteen had failed to set up any force at all. The forces which did exist varied enormously in size and efficiency. By 1881 there remained thirty police forces with less than six men.

1856 County and Borough Police Act

In 1856, a new Act was passed to increase the uniformity and efficiency of the various police forces and to enhance the control of the Home Office. The 1856 County and Borough Police Act

- Required magistrates in all counties to maintain a police force.
- Required the justices (of every county) and watch committees (of every borough) to report annually to the Home Secretary on the number of offences reported in their area, the number of

arrests, the nature of the charges, the results of proceedings, etc., a summary of which would be laid before Parliament.
- Empowered the Home Secretary to appoint three inspectors to visit county and borough forces to assess their efficiency and report to him, the reports being laid before Parliament.
- Empowered central government to pay one quarter of the cost of the pay and clothing of local forces *if* the inspectors judged them efficient. Forces serving a population under 5,000 would not be eligible.

A clause extending to the boroughs the Home Secretary's power to make the rules governing local forces (thus depriving the watch committees of that power) was withdrawn from the Bill in face of opposition.

The Home Secretary was nevertheless able to exercise considerable influence over all the local forces through his power to withhold the one-quarter grant from those not judged efficient (a grant later increased to half) — a course of action which is known to have been threatened, on average, once a year during the period 1885-1900. In Worcester, for instance, in 1857, soon after the passing of the Act, the watch committee reported that its force had been inspected by a General Cartright, who did not consider the force efficient. Amongst other things, he suggested that the size of the force should be increased by six men. Without such an increase, the city would not get the government grant. The cost of maintaining the force with the proposed increase, it was reported, was £1,519 16s, less the government grant of £380 (one quarter).[14]

Some police authorities (the collective term for watch committees and quarter sessions of justices) resented the inspections so much that they refused the grant when offered.

The inspectors strongly encouraged the amalgamation of small borough forces with county forces, a proposal which the Worcester city watch committee deemed 'an unconstitutional interference with the rights and privileges of Corporations, so depriving the citizens of the control of the police, the expense of which they are required to defray, and for the efficiency of which they are responsible'.[15]

The new inspectorate is credited nevertheless with formulating, for the first time, national policing policies based on the information and experience they collected on their inspections. Reporting to the Home Secretary, the inspectorate put his department in a position to plan developments and policies throughout the country.

The inspectorate was given no authority to inspect the Metropolitan Police, an anomaly which persists today.

Political Control v. Judicial Independence

Democratic local government finally reached the counties in 1888 when the Local Government Act established county councils. But control of the county police forces was not transferred to a watch committee of the council to bring the position into line with that in the boroughs. The justices clung to their powers and, to justify their position, raised the (now familiar) argument that the police should be under their authority rather than that of elected representatives, because they were not subject to the dangers of political bias. As a compromise, 'standing joint committees' were established with an equal number of councillors and magistrates; this completed the administrative system which was to remain more or less intact in the counties until 1964. The Act reiterated the stipulation that constables had to obey the lawful orders of justices, but again it remained unclear who was actually to control the police. Critchley suggests that the effect of the Act was to increase the power of chief constables in the counties:

> . . . as the justices dropped out of the picture the contenders for power were chief constables and local police authorities; and the county men, with their generally greater social acceptability, wider powers of command over the force and looser subordination to the standing joint committee, slipped easily into a dominating position to which their borough colleagues could scarcely aspire without colliding with the watch committee.[16]

In contrast, in the boroughs the watch committees had sole responsibility for appointments, promotions and discipline, and for drawing up the regulations for the force, without the countervailing Home Office powers to which the joint standing committees were subject. Consequently, their chief constables had fewer powers and a lower social status than their counterparts in the counties. Critchley suggests that it often suited a watch committee to appoint

> . . . a local man of quiet and tractable disposition; and, as the appointment was not subject to the approval of the Home Secretary, no one could prevent a mischievous town council from exercising improper pressure on its police. It could use them to support groups of local trades people, sectional interests or political parties, and where the population was under 5,000 (and hence no Exchequer grant was payable) no threat to

withhold a grant was available to bring redemptive influence to bear.[17]

In towns where publicans and brewers had considerable influence, for example, the watch committee would insist that the police did not take any licensee to court without their permission. The Chief Constable of Norwich was, in fact, dismissed for defying such a ruling.

While the county chief constable was 'supreme commander of his force and acknowledged little authority', the borough man was '"merely the superintending and executive officer of the watch committee". In other words the counter-part of the County Chief Constable was the watch committee itself, not the head constable of the borough'.[18]

Home Office files contain a memo dated 1876 which confirms this view:

> the head constable of a borough police force holds an inferior position as compared with the chief constable of a county force. In fact, in a borough, the watch committee, subject to the council, discharges several of the functions which with respect to a county police force belong to the chief constable or the secretary of state.[19]

This anomaly was not rectified until the watch committees and joint standing committees were replaced and a uniform system of control imposed (except in London) by the 1964 Police Act.

Chief Constables Clash with Watch Committees

Conflicts inevitably arose between watch committees and their chief constables, for while the committees continued to expect their chief officers to follow their instructions, chief constables increasingly insisted on their autonomy in enforcing the law. Moreover, some justices insisted on their independent right to issue instructions. Those few conflicts which are recorded illustrate, but did not resolve, this ambiguous relationship.

In Birmingham, for example, in 1880, the chief constable clashed with the local justices when he decided that all drunks should be taken into custody and brought before a justice, thus reversing the previous policy not to interfere unless the drunks were disorderly. The justices, and members of the public, criticised the decision and the chief constable withdrew it. The following year, however, he clashed with his watch committee when he (unsuccessfully) prosecuted the manager of a music hall, alleging improper performance and performing plays without a licence.[20] The watch committee rejected his claim to an independent right to initiate prosecutions, and resolved that he should not take proceedings 'likely to affect a number of ratepayers or to provoke public comment' without letting them know in advance.

The chief constable refused to comply with this instruction unless ordered to do so by the Home Secretary or the justices, but the Home Secretary refused to intervene, simply reminding him of the watch committee's power to make regulations to ensure the efficiency of the force and to dismiss officers who were negligent or otherwise unfit. Similarly the justices, while asserting their authority and control over the police, chose not to interfere. In face of a council resolution that it was undesirable to retain the services of a chief officer of police who was 'not subordinate to or not in harmony with' the watch committee, the chief constable complied.

On another occasion, in 1902, when the Chief Constable of Margate was caught in the cross-fire of a political struggle between the justices and the watch committee, the conflict took a different course. The chief constable was faced with conflicting instructions from the justices, who ordered him to take proceedings against certain publicans, and the watch committee, which instructed him not to serve the summonses. The justices then threatened to suspend him for neglect of duty in failing to carry out their instructions. The chief constable considered his position intolerable and resigned, although not until the justices had finally backed down.

Neither of these disputes resolved the question as to whether or not the chief constable was in fact entitled to act independently in enforcing the law. In the Birmingham incident, although the chief constable finally complied with the watch committee's instructions, the committee had not demanded the right to instruct him, only to be informed of his intentions with respect to certain kinds of prosecution. The justices, on the other hand, although they chose not to intervene, re-asserted their right to do so. The Home Secretary chose to remind the chief constable of the watch committee's supervisory power over him, but did not suggest that the committee had any right to instruct him. In Margate, where the conflict hinged on the watch committee's and justices' rights to instruct the chief constable, the chief constable chose to resign rather than comply with the instructions of either the committee or the JPs.

While, as we shall see, it is undoubtedly true that watch committees did exercise greater power over the police than police authorities do now, it is *not* accurate to say that they had a statutory right to instruct their chief constable. Rather, the law at that time was sufficiently ambiguous to allow a variety of practices — from the virtual independence of the chief constable through to daily supervision by the watch committee, all of which were equally within the law. What determined the outcome of conflicts was not the law but the degree of political influence wielded by the different authorities responsible for law enforcement, which was affected by such factors as the social standing (and thus authority) of the chief constable and the extent to which the Home Secretary was willing (or felt able) to intervene.[21]

The absence of disputes in the counties, far from being the result of county chief constables following the instructions of the joint standing committees, was due to the committees' willingness to give the chief constables a free hand in running their forces, coupled with their greater powers regarding the appointment and discipline of their men.

Home Office Increases Its Influence

Developments in policing in the early part of the twentieth century were marked by a steady increase in Home Office influence, without a commensurate extension of its accountability to Parliament. The two world wars had a significant influence on this process. But the indication that central government was increasing its influence at the expense of local decision-making came before the beginning of the First World War, when the Welsh miners demonstrated in Tonypandy in 1910.

Winston Churchill, then Home Secretary, showed in the handling of the disturbances how the old principle of local responsibility for law enforcement could be abandoned overnight in face of a forceful Home Secretary.[22] Having arranged for troops to stand by, Churchill sent hundreds of mounted and foot Metropolitan Police officers by train to Tonypandy to back up the local chief constable, directing the operation himself from his office in London.

It was during the First World War, however, that the police really got used to receiving instructions from the Home Office under the emergency regulations passed to co-ordinate wartime operations. For the first time, direct links were forged between the Home Office and chief constables, who began to meet regularly at the Home Office to discuss all aspects of policing policy and practice, which led in turn to closer co-operation between forces and mutual sharing of ideas. The Home Office issued advisory circulars and organised conferences and working parties, thus beginning the process of unifying the disparate forces within a federal structure and, sometimes in face of local opposition, standardising force policies and practices.

Widespread discontent and unrest within the police forces, due to low pay and poor working conditions, resulted in an unprecedented strike by London's police in 1918, which led indirectly to the acquisition of greater powers by the Home Office. The Desborough Committee,[23] set up in 1919 to resolve police grievances, recommended a number of changes, enacted in the 1919 Police Act, which significantly increased the role of the Home Secretary. It introduced a 'new concept of a centrally guided and largely uniform system of local police forces'.[24]

The Home Secretary was now responsible for standardising pay and conditions throughout the force; the resulting series of increases in police pay was to mark the beginning of their professional status. A Police Council was established as an advisory body to the Home Secretary, with representatives from all ranks and from police authorities, and police 'unions' were formed to negotiate with the Home Office on pay and conditions. Finally, and perhaps most significantly, the financial contribution from central government to each force was increased to *half* the total cost of maintaining the police force. A new Police Department was organised within the Home Office to administer its new responsibilities. The Home Secretary was not required to submit his new regulations to Parliament for its approval.

Bunyan suggests that it was not coincidence that this centralisation of control over the police occurred during the same period that the working class were given the vote and Labour Party councillors were beginning to form majorities on councils.[25]

By the beginning of the Second World War the Home Office had

. . . built up a position of quite remarkable influence in police affairs . . . the prolific 'advice' and 'guidance' contained in the Home Office circulars on all manner of subjects became a euphemism for 'direction'; and chief constables, resentful of any attempt at interference from outside, would look to an informal exchange with the Home Office to settle almost any problem. Thus, for good or ill, the department had worked itself into a position of exercising great power without formal responsibility . . .[26]

The Second World War gave further impetus to this trend. Although the police were not, like the fire service, nationalised, temporary Defence Regulations empowered the Home Secretary to instruct both chief constables and police authorities and, 'although the Home Office was not formally constituted as a Ministry of Police, there are times when it acted like one . . .'[27]

This line of command ceased in 1945 but the Home Office continued to extend its influence in other areas, in particular through training — establishing a national police college and district training centres — and by compelling small forces to amalgamate (under the 1946 Police Act), thus reducing the number of forces in England and Wales to 125 by 1962.

The Royal Commission on the Police

A series of controversial incidents in the late 1950s highlighted the ambiguity in the law governing the relationship between the police and elected representatives and brought into question the adequacy of the means of calling the police to account. In contrast to the current debate on police accountability, however, the immediate focus of concern then was not policing policies *per se* but the actions, and misdemeanours, of individual police officers. Nevertheless, the incidents, which led to the appointment of the Royal Commission in 1960, raised questions which are still pertinent today.

Possibly the most serious incident was that in Nottingham in 1958 where the chief constable was suspended by his watch committee, only to be reinstated by the Home Secretary. It occurred in the wake of a series of corruption scandals, implicating no lesser figures than the Chief Constables of Brighton and, in a separate incident, of Worcester.

Nottingham watch committee clashed with its chief constable when it asked him to report on enquiries he had instigated into allegations that members of the council had acted corruptly. He argued that it was his duty, and not that of the watch committee, to enforce the criminal law, and refused to comply. The committee suspended him, using its powers under the 1835 Act, as unfit for office. But the Home Secretary, unlike his predecessor in the Birmingham case, supported the chief constable's stand and reinstated him.

In doing so, the Home Secretary relied on a series of court judgements (in particular *Fisher* v. *Oldham Corporation* (1930)[28] and *The Attorney General for New South Wales* v. *Perpetual Trustee Company* (1955), an Australian case that turned on English law[29] — see chapter 2), which had held that the constable's powers were derived from common law and were not delegated; he was not, therefore, the servant of the police authority or the Crown. Nevertheless, the implications of these judgements for the status of chief constables were not clear, and the incident served mainly to highlight the contradiction between the judgements and the power possessed by the watch committees to dismiss a constable considered unfit for duty.

The case which precipitated the appointment of the Royal Commission was that of *Garratt* v. *Eastmond*,[30] when the Metropolitan Commissioner used public funds to settle an action for assault and false imprisonment, taken by Mr Garratt against PC Eastmond, without accepting liability. When it was later announced that no disciplinary proceedings would be taken against PC Eastmond, there was an outcry. MPs asked why £300 of public money had been spent if PC Eastmond had not been at fault? If he had been, why had he not been disciplined?

The Home Secretary replied by announcing the establishment of a Royal Commission. According to Critchley, who was appointed Clerk to the Commission, 'Its genesis was, basically, concern about the means of controlling the police and bringing them to account when things went wrong: in short, it was the need for a redefinition, acceptable to Parliament, of the constitutional position of the police in the State'.[31]

The Commission[32] was asked 'to review the constitutional position of the police throughout Great Britain, the arrangements for their control and administration'. In particular, it was to consider:

1. the constitution and function of local police authorities;
2. the status and accountability of members of police forces, including chief officers of police;
3. the relationship of the police with the public and the means of ensuring that complaints by the public against the police are effectively dealt with; and
4. the broad principles which should govern the remuneration of the constable, having regard to the nature and extent of police duties and responsibilities and the need to attract and retain an adequate number of recruits with the proper qualifications.

The fourth of these points was the subject of an interim report by the Commission and led to a substantial increase in police pay.

It is significant that the Royal Commission's stated objective was to devise a system of control which would enable the police to carry out their duties impartially and with maximum efficiency, while ensuring an adequate means of calling the police to account, to keep a 'proper check upon mistakes and errors of judgement'. It did not include among its objectives ensuring that policing policies reflected the needs and priorities of the communities they served.

Consequently, the recommendations the Commission devised did not reflect this requirement.

The evidence which the Royal Commission received led it to believe that the objectives it had identified were not met by the existing system. And it further highlighted the confusion in the law which recent events had illustrated.

While chief constables asserted their complete independence from local control in enforcing the law,[33] the Association of Municipal Corporations claimed that police authorities *could* give chief constables instructions, for example on their methods of dealing with a political demonstration, although it said they should not interfere in the application of the criminal law in particular cases. The fact that police authorities delegated executive control to chief constables was, it argued, a matter of good administrative practice rather than of law. It thought the current legal position satisfactory and sought no change.[34]

The Commission, however, thought the position thoroughly unsatisfactory and marvelled that it had worked with relatively little conflict for so long. The solution it clearly favoured initially was to increase central control over the police, and it presented a strong case for a national police force accountable to the Home Secretary. Unfortunately for the Commission, the vast majority of those who gave evidence to it did not agree.

The Commission's compromise was to devise recommendations which were 'based on a continuance of the idea of partnership between central and local government in the administration of the police service but with a shifting emphasis ... towards firmer control by central government'.[35]

The Commission recognised that the legal status of the police, in denying that they are the servants of the Crown or of a police authority, '... accords them a position of exceptional independence. It follows that they are subject to little legal control in carrying out their duties'.[36] It noted that, like everyone else, the police have to obey the law, but commented that this provided no guidance on *how* to enforce it.

Nevertheless, the Commission assumed that the discipline and complaints procedure was adequate to control the majority of officers and concluded: 'The problem of controlling the police can, therefore, be restated as the problem of controlling chief constables'.[37] The chief constable, the Commission noted,

> ... is accountable to no one, and subject to no one's orders, for the way in which, for example, he settles his general policies in respect to law enforcement over the area covered by his force, the disposition of his force, the concentration of his resources on

any particular type of crime or area, the manner in which he handles political demonstrations or processions, and allocates and instructs his men when preventing breaches of the peace arising from industrial disputes, the methods he employs in dealing with an outbreak of violence or of passive resistance to authority, his policy in enforcing the traffic laws and in dealing with parked vehicles, and so on,[38]

and it questioned whether he should remain immune from external control in formulating and applying policies of this kind 'which vitally concern the public interest'.[39] Moreover, should not the community, through its elected representatives, have some say in the maintenance of law and order?

The Commission concluded that chief constables ought to 'be subject to more effective supervision', but believed:

The problem is to move towards this objective without compromising the chief constable's impartiality in enforcing the law in particular cases.[40]

. . . to achieve the advantage of preserving their impartiality as regards some activities, with the advantage of placing them under a degree of external supervision as regards others: more narrowly, it is to provide effective means of redress against inefficiency or bias while not hindering the efficient and impartial chief constable.[41]

Here again, the Commission juxtaposed police impartiality on the one hand with the danger of political interference on the other. Its priority was to preserve police impartiality, while devising a mechanism for calling to account an inefficient chief constable, rather than to ensure that the public were able to influence policing policies and methods. The solution it devised, reflecting these assumptions and priorities, was to maintain the chief constable's independence, but to make him liable to give account of his actions afterwards: 'while the chief constable would continue to enjoy immunity from orders he would nevertheless be exposed to advice and guidance of which he would be expected to take heed'.[42]

The Commission recommended that police authorities should have four main duties:

- to provide and equip an adequate police force;
- to constitute a body able to advise chief constables on local conditions;

- to appoint, discipline and remove senior officers from the force; and
- to play an active role in fostering good relations between the police and the public.[43]

However, it recommended that the legal responsibility for the efficient policing of the area should be taken from police authorities and given to the Home Secretary, in line with its belief that local forces 'should be brought under more effective central control'. Consequently it recommended that police authorities be given limited powers to enable them to carry out the following functions:

- Calling for reports from chief constables on matters related to policing, a function which (in relation to that already existing in Scotland) it had previously described as 'limited in scope. It affords an opportunity for the expression of anxiety by the local community or the central authority about the trend of a chief constable's actions; but it does not provide a direct means of checking or alerting them'.[44] Moreover, it recommended that chief constables be entitled to refuse to provide a report, subject to the approval of the Home Secretary.
- Appointing and dismissing their chief constables and their deputies (subject again to the approval of the Home Secretary). Once again, it had described the latter function as having 'only a regulative effect . . . they were obviously not intended to be instruments for compelling a change of policy by a chief constable on a relatively minor matter; nor are they appropriate for that purpose'.[45]
- Requisitioning police expenditure from their local councils.

All police authorities should, the Commission thought, be comprised of two thirds councillors and one third justices, with a councillor in the chair. The Commission did not resolve the question of whether justices should retain their independent powers but suggested that these should be reviewed. And it recommended that the watch committees' powers to appoint, promote and discipline the subordinate ranks be transferred to chief constables.

Although recommending that the Home Secretary be made legally responsible for the efficiency of the police, the Commission did not argue that he should have the power to direct chief constables. Rather, it noted approvingly the extensive influence that the Home Office had been able to achieve via administrative devices, in particular its frequent circulars with which 'a chief constable would hesitate to press disagreement'.[46] What was wrong with this situation, the Commission felt, was that, despite exercising such extensive influence, the Home Secretary was not answerable to Parliament for the exercise of most of his powers. This situation could be remedied by making him *legally* responsible for policing, and hence accountable to Parliament for the way in which he exercised his powers.

The Commission proposed that the Secretary of State be given the power to call for reports on policing from chief constables and that his existing powers over local forces be enhanced, in particular those relating to the amalgamation of forces, the appointment and dismissal of chief constables, and the size and effectiveness of the Inspectorate of Constabulary. This would enable him to meet 'the need for a more vigorous lead from the centre'.[47]

Finally, the Commission recommended that the Home Secretary remain the police authority for London. Having heard 'little evidence critical of the general principle embodied in these arrangements', it simply argued that 'in view of the exceptional police responsibilities in London, control should be in the hands of the Government'.[48] For the City of London, it saw policing problems which were 'unique and specialised', but hesitated to say that these conditions necessitated a separate police force and separate police authority. However, having heard no unfavourable evidence about the existing system, it recommended no change.[49]

Conclusion

The early history of the police reveals no clear trend towards, or away from, accountability to elected representatives. Moreover, even if watch committees and their rural counterparts had controlled the police to a greater extent this could not, it has to be said, have been called democratic accountability. Prior to this century, the majority of the population most affected by policing were not allowed to vote.

The common and statutory law governing the relationship between the different parties — chief constables, justices, councillors and the Home Secretary — remained ambiguous, a compromise between the conflicting interests of these parties and the classes they represented. The outcome of the conflicts which arose was determined not by the law but by the relative political influence of those involved in each situation — hence the differing outcomes in each case. We cannot, therefore, cite any one incident and say 'this shows that watch committees did control the police' or, alternatively, 'this shows that, when the cards were down, chief constables were autonomous and could make their own decisions'. The failure of this system to maintain adequate control over the police led to the establishment of the Royal Commission.

The Royal Commission on the Police did not seek to devise arrangements for controlling the police which would ensure that policing policies reflected the wishes of the communities they served. It identified its objective as to devise institutional arrangements which would increase control over chief constables without endangering their impartiality. It believed it would be far more beneficial to increase the central control of the Home Office than to increase the role of local government.

The intention behind the Commission's recommendations was thus to shift responsibility for the efficiency of the police (a term which, incidentally, was never defined) from police authorities to central government. The Home Secretary was to be responsible for that efficiency, and he was to be accountable to Parliament for the way in which he exercised his powers. Police authorities, perceived as advice-giving committees, were to be given few powers.

When the Police Bill was published in 1963, it embodied almost all the Commission's recommendations. But one fundamental proposal, on which the whole package rested, was omitted: *responsibility* for the efficiency of each separate force was to remain with the local police authority and not be given to the Home Secretary. Nevertheless, the respective *powers* of each were to be very much as the Commission proposed.

The implication of this crucial change was this: on the one hand police authorities would be responsible for maintaining an efficient force but have few powers to ensure this efficiency; on the other hand the Home Secretary would have the power to exert considerable influence over the police, but his officials could exercise this influence behind closed doors with impunity.

For the Home Secretary can only be called to account by MPs for those aspects of policing for which he has statutory responsibility. While his officials are, in theory, accountable through him to Parliament for all their actions, Home Secretaries can and do refuse to answer questions from MPs on any policy matter for which they have no statutory responsibility, replying that 'this is a matter for the chief constable' or 'for the police authority'. Hence, any influence which the Home Office exerts beyond its direct statutory responsibilities is not subject to scrutiny by Parliament.

By rejecting the Commission's central proposal but accepting the rest of the package, the government thus set up a system in which police authorities have wide responsibilities but few powers and central government exercises enormous influence for which it is rarely accountable. The Act came into force on 1 June 1965.

Notes

1. T.A. Critchley, *A History of Police in England and Wales* (Constable, revised edition 1978), p.19.
2. *Report of the Select Committee on the Police of the Metropolis* (17 June 1822). Quoted in Critchley, *op.cit.*, p.47. Opposition to a Bill proposing a paid professional police force for the City of London many years earlier had resulted in the Bill being transferred to Ireland, where it became the Dublin Police Act of 1786. The Royal Irish Constabulary was formed in 1836.
3. J.L. Lyman, 'The Metropolitan Police Act 1829', *Journal of Criminal Law, Criminology and Political Science*, Vol.55 (1964).
4. *Ibid.*, pp.151-2.
5. Mr Henry Mathews, 330 HC Deb, 3rd Ser. Col.1, 174 (Hansard), quoted in Critchley, *op.cit.*, p.268.
6. Critchley, *op.cit.*, p.56.
7. *Ibid.*, p.54.
8. *Ibid.*, p.66.
9. Michael Brogden, *The Police: Autonomy and Consent* (Academic Press, 1982), pp.62-71. Brogden found in his research that the subcommittee's instructions arose directly from the requests for police help made by local property holders and shopkeepers — 'the wealthy elite and associated trading class'. Ninety per cent of the requests were for the police to control the streets and recreational premises (bars, brothels) — to demarcate the territories of the poor: 'The Watch Committee', he writes, 'was little more than a conduit through which class demands were articulated into practice'.
10. Quoted in Critchley, *op.cit.*, p.78.
11. 1839 County Police Act.
12. Critchley, *op.cit.*, p.80.
13. *The Times*, 26 July 1839.
14. 'Worcester City Police', *The Marches* Issue 7 1981 (the official magazine of the West Mercia Police). Based on research by Chief Superintendent Colin Glover.
15. *Ibid*.
16. Critchley, *op.cit.*, p.138.
17. *Ibid.*, p.125.
18. *Ibid.*, p.143, quoting in agreement a memo from the Chief Constable of Norfolk to the Home Secretary in 1858.
19. Quoted in Critchley, *op.cit.*, p.143.
20. *Ibid.*, p.131.
21. See Tony Jefferson and Roger Grimshaw, *Controlling the Constable* (Muller/Cobden Trust, 1984), chapter 2.
22. Critchley, *op.cit.*, p.179.
23. *Report of Committee on the Police Service of England and Wales* (1919), HMSO 29.
24. Critchley, *op.cit.*, p.194.
25. Tony Bunyan, *The History and Practice of the Political Police in Britain* (Quartet, 1977), p.72.
26. Critchley, *op.cit.*, p.219.
27. *Ibid.*, p.223.
28. *Fisher v. Oldham Corporation* [1930] 2 KB 364.
29. *Attorney General for New South Wales v. Perpetual Trustee Company (and others)* [1955] AC 457.
30. *Garratt v. Eastmond* (unreported), see *The Times*, 18 November 1959, and Hansard, 18 November 1959, cols.1239-1303.
31. Critchley, *op.cit.*, p.274.

32. *Report of the Royal Commission on the Police* (HMSO, May 1962), Cmnd 1728.
33. *Ibid.*, para.72.
34. *Ibid.*, para.76.
35. *Ibid.*, para.23.
36. *Ibid.*, para.100.
37. *Ibid.*, para.102.
38. *Ibid.*, para.89.
39. *Ibid.*, para.90.
40. *Ibid.*, para.92.
41. *Ibid.*, para.102.
42. *Ibid.*, para.93.
43. *Ibid.*, para.480(ii).
44. *Ibid.*, para.108.
45. *Ibid.*, para.108.
46. *Ibid.*, para.113.
47. *Ibid.*, para.293.
48. *Ibid.*, para.222.
49. *Ibid.*, para.228.

CHAPTER 2
The Police and Elected Representatives (1): The Law

Recommending his new Police Bill to Parliament in 1963 the then Conservative Home Secretary told the House: 'One of the lessons of modern times is that a police system, instituted to defend freedom and maintain law and order, must itself be under effective control'.[1] The Bill, he said, aimed 'to bring the police under more effective supervision'. It would ensure that the chief constable 'is fully accountable for what he does'.[2]

But the Bill, which was 'generally' welcomed by the Labour opposition, gave neither elected representatives nor the courts the power to *control* the police. Nor did it ensure that they would be accountable for their actions.

Although one of the problems in the past had been the uncertainty surrounding the respective powers of chief constables, magistrates and elected representatives, the 1964 Police Act in fact perpetuated this uncertainty. Locally elected representatives are given wide responsibilities but few powers with which to fulfil them; while some of their powers overlap with those of their chief constable so that it is unclear who has the final say. Moreover, many of their decisions are subject to a veto by the chief constable or the Home Secretary.

The Act replaced the old dual system of watch committees and joint standing committees with a single system of committees known as 'police authorities'. Outside London, police authorities consist of two thirds councillors, appointed by the council for the area covered by the force, and one third magistrates.

Where a force covers more than one county, such as Thames Valley (which covers Berkshire, Oxfordshire and Buckinghamshire), a combined police authority was to be formed with councillors and magistrates from each county. There are forty-one police authorities in England and Wales (outside

London), thirty-one relating to single counties and ten combined authorities.

In London, the situation is quite different. There are two forces: the Metropolitan Police, the largest force in the country, for which the police authority is the Home Secretary alone, and the City of London force, for which the police authority is the Common Council of the City of London.[3]

The 1964 Act extended the powers of the Home Secretary and of chief constables, at the expense of the provincial police authorities. Most of the powers of appointment, promotion, discipline and dismissal which the old watch committees had enjoyed were transferred to chief constables, and any claim which watch committees and magistrates might once have had that they had the right to tell their chief constable how to enforce the law was silenced by putting the force under his sole 'direction and control'.

The government's stated intention in introducing the new Act was that 'the Police Authority will be responsible for providing an efficient instrument and supervising its use. The chief constable will be responsible for using that instrument efficiently'.[4] It believed that it was possible to draw a distinction between administrative/financial decisions, which could be made by the police authority, and 'operational' decisions, which should be made by the chief constable. It wrote this distinction into the Act as responsibility for 'efficiency' and 'direction and control' respectively. It was accepted that locally and nationally elected representatives should make financial decisions because of their responsibility to the rate/tax payers to spend their money wisely. But there was no recognition in the Act that many other policing decisions are political and therefore ought also to be made by elected representatives.

The government's stated intention was to leave it to the chief constable's discretion how he enforced the law. It was hoped that police authorities would give their chief constables advice but they were given no authority to tell them what to do. This relationship is, as the Royal Commission on the Police had recommended it should be, the reverse of that between other local government committees and their chief officers.[5] The Royal Commission devised a unique formula to place chief officers 'under a degree of external supervision' while 'preserving their impartiality': this was to give them the power to decide how to enforce the law but to make them liable to give an account of (some of) their actions afterwards to their police authority and the Home Secretary. This formula was embodied in the Act and, as the Home Office sees it:

the system which now exists for controlling the police thus

involves the inter-relationship of three authorities — the Home Secretary, the local police authorities and the chief officers of police — in a complex relationship which ensures that *except in respect of day-to-day operations*, no one of the three has absolute control [our emphasis].[6]

Finally, the Act gave the Home Secretary the power to amalgamate police forces, a power which was used extensively during the early years of the Act, reducing the total number of forces in England and Wales from 125 in 1962 to forty-three now. Although the reason for the amalgamations was to increase efficiency, the effect was also to increase the distance between the public and these larger, more remote forces; to increase the power of senior officers, who now commanded larger forces; and to necessitate the establishment of the ten joint police authorities, which have a less direct relationship of accountability with their county councils and the public.

Powers and Duties of Police Authorities

Police authorities outside London are committees of the county council but their powers are not delegated from the council, as is the case with other local government committees, but directly from statute — the 1964 Act.[7] This states that:

> it shall be the duty of the police authority . . . to secure the maintenance of an adequate and efficient police force for their area, and to exercise for that purpose the powers conferred on a police authority by this Act (s.4(a)).

In addition police authorities must 'keep themselves informed as to the manner in which complaints made by members of the public against members of a police force are dealt with by the chief constable' (s.50).

To fulfil their responsibilities, police authorities have the power to:

- Appoint the chief constable of the force and determine the number of persons of each rank, *subject to the approval of the Home Secretary* and any regulation he may make (see below regarding regulations) (s.4(2)).
- Appoint the deputy and assistant chief constables after consulting with the chief constable and *subject to the approval of the Home Secretary* (s.6(4)).

- Call on the chief constable, assistant or deputy chief constable to retire in the interests of efficiency, *with the approval of the Home Secretary* (s.5(4)).
- Provide, maintain and make alterations to buildings, structures, and premises required by the force — *subject to the consent of the Home Secretary* (s.4(3)).
- Provide and maintain vehicles, apparatus, clothing and other equipment required by the force, *subject to any regulations made by the Home Secretary* (s.4(4)).
- Act as the disciplinary authority for the chief constable, deputy and assistant chief constable (s.33(3)(a)).
- Require its chief constable to submit a report in writing on matters connected with the policing of the area (s.12(2)).

However:

> If it appears to the chief constable that a report in compliance with any such requirement of the police authority would contain information which in the public interest ought not to be disclosed, or is not needed for the discharge of the functions of the police authority, he may request that authority to refer the requirement to the Secretary of State; and in any such case the requirement shall be of no effect unless it is confirmed by the Secretary of State (s.12(3)).

If the police authority receives a report from its chief constable with which it is dissatisfied, it is given no powers to *instruct* him to change any of his operational policing policies or practices.

In order to fulfil its responsibility for maintaining an efficient force, the authority determines the police budget, subject (except in the case of combined authorities) to the approval of the full council, which obtains the money from the rates. The remainder is paid by central government, *if* the Home Secretary deems the force 'efficient'. As we shall see, this financial control by the Home Office reduces the degree of control over the force of both the police authority and the chief constable. Certain items of expenditure, such as police salaries, are also determined in advance by the Home Office (after negotiations with police representatives).

Finally, the Police Act states that a police authority maintaining a police force to which aid is provided by another force must pay to the aiding authority 'such contribution as may be agreed between those authorities'. If they cannot agree, the Home Secretary determines the sum to be paid (s.14(4)).

In London, the Home Secretary alone is the police authority for the Metropolitan Police. The powers of the Home Secretary as police authority are, however, greater than those of his provincial counterparts. The 1964 Police Act did not alter this role, which was established by the 1829 Metropolitan Police Act; s.5 of that Act requiring the Commissioner of Police of the Metropolis (or 'Metropolitan Commissioner', as he is generally known) to submit to the Home Secretary any orders he makes for the force.

The Home Secretary's other powers as a police authority, for example to call for reports, are the same as those of police authorities in the rest of the country.

No locally elected representatives in London, whether councillors or Members of Parliament, thus have any direct responsibility for policing the metropolis or control over how the share of the cost raised from the rates is spent.

The Police and Criminal Evidence Act[8] places an additional responsibility on police authorities outside London to 'make arrangements' to get the views of the public on the policing of their area and to obtain their co-operation in helping the police prevent crime. The nature and extent of these 'arrangements' are not defined and the consultative committees, if any are established, have no statutory powers. Each authority must consult its chief constable 'as to the arrangements that would be appropriate', and review the arrangements from time to time.

In London, highlighting the different role of the Home Secretary as the police authority, the responsibility for making such arrangements is placed on the Metropolitan Commissioner. He has a duty to make separate arrangements in each borough and, in doing so, must consult each borough council and take account of any guidance issued by the Home Secretary.[9]

If the Home Secretary considers that the arrangements are not adequate in any area he can insist that they are reviewed and require reports to be submitted to him by the authority (or Metropolitan Commissioner) until he is satisfied.

Powers of the Full Council

The council, within which the police authority is known as the 'police committee', has no direct responsibility for policing. Its powers are limited to:

(a) appointing the councillor members of the authority (s.2(2));
(b) approving its expenditure (s.8) — except in the case of combined police authorities. Combined police authorities have the power to precept their constituent county councils, which cannot control their expenditure. No county council can veto police

authority expenditure if it is required to implement government regulations or to discharge any statutory duty. (This covers the greater part of the police budget, which is taken up by police pay.)
(c) questioning the authority's nominated representatives at council meetings on the way in which the authority has discharged its responsibilities (s.11).

Powers and Duties of Chief Constables

Each police force is under the 'direction and control' of its chief constable (s.5(1)), who has a statutory duty to enforce the law. Under the 1964 Act, the chief constable has the power to appoint, promote and discipline all officers up to the rank of chief superintendent and is required to investigate all complaints against any of his officers.

Each year, he (they are all men) must submit a written report to his police authority and to the Home Secretary on the policing of the area (s.12(1)). Additionally, as we have seen, he must submit other reports as requested during the year to the police authority, unless he thinks that this would be against the public interest or is not necessary to enable the police authority to fulfil its responsibility for maintaining the 'efficiency' of the force. If he does refuse, the Home Secretary is the arbiter.

'Efficiency' is not defined in the Act, so this clause effectively leaves it to chief constables and the Home Secretary to decide how widely, or narrowly, the police authorities' responsibility should be defined.

A chief constable can, at the request of another chief constable, provide 'aid' to that force in the form of constables or other assistance (s.14(1)).

Powers and Duties of the Home Secretary

The Home Secretary does not share the police authority's statutory responsibility for the efficiency of each force (except for the Metropolitan Police, for which he is the police authority) but must 'exercise his powers . . . in such a manner and to such an extent as appears to him to be best calculated to promote the efficiency of the police' (s.28).

The powers which the Act gives him are extensive. Apart from supervising the exercise of (most of) the police authorities' powers he may:

- Pay 50 per cent of the cost of each force if he is satisfied that the area is efficiently policed and withhold all or part of the grant if he is not satisfied.[10]
- Require a police authority to call upon its chief constable to retire in the interests of efficiency (s.29(1)).
- Require any chief constable to submit a report to him on the policing of his area (s.30(1)).
- Order a local enquiry into any matter connected with the policing of any area (s.32(1)).
- Make regulations 'as to the government, administration, and conditions of service of police forces' (s.33) including: ranks to be held by members of police forces; qualifications required for appointment and promotion; periods of service on probation; voluntary retirement; maintenance of discipline; suspension of officers from their force and from their office as constables; maintenance of personal records of members of the force; duties which are, or are not, to be performed; the hours of duty, leave, pay, and allowances.
- Make regulations regarding special constables, police cadets, (s.32 and s.35) and requiring equipment used by the police to satisfy certain standards of design and performance (s.36). These important regulations do not need to be debated in Parliament; they are simply laid before Parliament and could be rejected by a majority vote in either House (s.33(6)).
- Determine, with the approval of the Treasury, the number of Inspectors of Constabulary, who have a duty 'to inspect, and report to the Secretary of State on the efficiency of all police forces' except the Metropolitan Police (s.38), and 'to carry out such other duties for the purpose of furthering police efficiency as the Secretary of State may from time to time direct' (s.38(3)). In addition, the Inspectorate must, like police authorities, keep itself informed about the way in which police complaints are being dealt with. The Chief Inspector must submit an annual report to the Home Secretary and this must be laid before Parliament (s.38(4)).

Finally, the Home Secretary may:

- Provide and maintain many central services, including police colleges and training centres, forensic science laboratories, wireless depots, and research relevant to the efficiency of the police (s.41 and s.42).
- Make regulations prescribing the constitution and proceedings of the Police Federations, the bodies which represent the interests of members of the police force (s.44(3)).

- Direct a chief constable to provide mutual aid to another force (s.14(2)). If two police authorities cannot agree how much money the *aided* authority should pay to the *aiding* authority for the aid provided, the Home Secretary can determine the sum to be paid (s.14(4)).

The Home Secretary is also the appeal body for officers found guilty of disciplinary offences (s.37).

The Home Secretary has no statutory duty to advise chief constables on how to exercise their powers, nor any general power to instruct them. The circulars which the Home Office issues to chief constables have no statutory authority, and the police are thus not obliged by law to observe them.

Members of Parliament may question the Home Secretary about policing matters for which he has *direct* responsibility. As the parameters of his direct responsibility are in practice unclear, so is the extent to which he can be obliged to answer.[11]

How the Courts Have Interpreted the Law

The extent of police authorities' powers under the 1964 Act has never been tested directly in the courts. But there has been a series of related judgements on the powers and responsibilities of police authorities and chief constables, which have consistently supported the independence of the police in enforcing the law.

In *Fisher* v. *Oldham Corporation* (1930),[12] for example, Fisher claimed that Oldham Corporation was responsible for his wrongful arrest by the police because it appointed the watch committee which was legally responsible for the police. The judge rejected the claim, arguing that the watch committee could not be liable as it had no power to tell any constable what to do. Moreover, he continued:

> If the local authorities are to be liable in such a case as this for the acts of the police with respect to felons and misdemeanours, then it would indeed be a serious matter and it would entitle them to demand that they ought to secure a full measure of control over the arrest and prosecution of all offenders. To give any such control would, in my view, involve a grave and most dangerous constitutional change.[13]

The second case which reinforced this view was that of *Attorney General for New South Wales* v. *Perpetual Trustee Company*

(1955),[14] a case which, although in Australia, relied on English law. Again, the issue was the relationship between the police authority and a constable and the judge concluded that the authority of the constable 'is original, not delegated, and is exercised at his own discretion by virtue of his office . . .'[15]

Perhaps the most famous judgements, however, are those arising from the cases brought by Raymond Blackburn against the Metropolitan Police Commissioner in which Blackburn alleged that the Commissioner was failing in his duty to prosecute, first, illegal gamblers, and then distributors of obscene material.

The first case, in 1968,[16] questioned whether the Commissioner could lawfully have a policy, in the form of a written instruction to his senior officers, not to take proceedings against clubs which breached the gaming laws, in certain circumstances. (Prior to the case reaching the Court of Appeal, the Commissioner withdrew the instruction.)

The Court of Appeal held that the Metropolitan Commissioner, and thereby chief constables, do have a duty to enforce the law, although they have some discretion over whether to prosecute in a particular case and over administrative matters. The courts would only intervene, however, if the police inaction amounted to a failure to enforce the law. In this case it would have intervened if the Commissioner had not already withdrawn the instruction.

In perhaps the most important judgement on police independence in relation to law enforcement, Lord Denning said of the Commissioner that, although his constitutional status had never been defined either by statute or the courts:

> I have no hesitation, however, in holding that, like every constable in the land, he should be, and is independent of the executive. He is not subject to the orders of the Secretary of State save that under the Police Act 1964 the Secretary of State can call on him to give a report, or to retire in the interests of efficiency.
>
> I hold it to be the duty of the Commissioner of Police, as it is of every chief constable, to enforce the law of the land. He must take steps so as to post his men that crimes may be detected; and that honest citizens may go about their affairs in peace. He must decide whether or not suspected persons are to be prosecuted, and, if need be, bring the prosecution or see that it is brought; but in all these things he is not the servant of anyone, save the law itself. No Minister of the Crown can tell him that he must, or must not, keep observation on this place or that; or that he must, or must not, prosecute this man or that one. Nor can any police authority tell him so. The responsibility for law

enforcement lies on him. He is answerable to the law and to the law alone.[17]

In a second case, in 1973,[18] the Commissioner's discretion as to whether and how to enforce the law was again the issue, but on this occasion there was no question of his having a definite policy not to do so. The judges were not uncritical of the approach that he had taken but were in agreement in reaffirming, in the words of Lord Justice Roskill, that

> It is no part of the duty of this court to presume to tell the respondent how to conduct the affairs of the Metropolitan Police, nor how to employ his all too limited resources at a time of ever-increasing crime, especially crimes of violence in London.[19]

And Lord Denning, drawing on his earlier judgement, held that

> ... in the carrying out of their duty of enforcing the law, the police have a discretion with which the courts will not interfere. There might, however, be extreme cases in which he was not carrying out his duty. And then we would. I do not think that is a case for our interference.[20]

The result of the two judgements was to emphasise that the police do have a duty to enforce the law. If they fail to do so, however, it is only in 'extreme' cases that the courts will intervene, and even then neither the courts nor the Home Secretary nor the police authorities have the right to tell a chief constable *how* to deploy his men. A more recent case has confirmed that the courts are very reluctant to intervene to compel the police to enforce the law.

In 1981 the Central Electricity Generating Board asked the Court of Appeal to instruct the Chief Constable of Devon and Cornwall to remove some demonstrators from the site of a potential nuclear power station which the CEGB wished to inspect. The chief constable had refused to intervene on the grounds that he had no statutory powers of arrest in the existing circumstances nor any common law powers of arrest as there had been no breach of the peace nor was any anticipated. Moreover, he argued, 'the police inevitably must maintain their low key presence to preserve the peace',[21] while his colleague, Chief Inspector Bradley, made the point that: 'If we involved ourselves in this context [community hostility to a proposed power station] our whole community relationship, which at the present time is second to none, and has taken a considerable length of time to establish, would be in jeopardy . . .'[22]

Lord Denning decided that the police did have a right to intervene (as the demonstrators were, in his view, causing a breach of the peace) and that they *should* have done so. Nevertheless, he would not order them to take action:

> Notwithstanding all that I have said I would not give orders to the chief constable or his men. It is of the first importance that the police should decide on their own responsibility what action should be taken in any particular situation . . . The decision of the chief constable not to intervene in this case was a policy decision with which I think the court should not interfere. All that I have done in this judgement is to give the 'definitive legal mandate' which he sought. It should enable him to reconsider his position. I hope he will decide to use his men to clear the obstructors off the site or at any rate help the board to do so.[23]

Notes

1. *Hansard*, 26 November 1963, col.83.
2. *Ibid.*, col. 84.
3. See chapter 2 for the historic reason for this anomaly.
4. *Hansard*, 26 November 1963, col.685.
5. See introduction.
6. 'Home Office Evidence to the Royal Commission on Criminal Procedure' (1978), Memorandum No.1, p.8.
7. The Act was amended by the 1972 Local Government Act, to take account of local government reorganisation, and by the 1976 Police Act, which changed the procedure for handling complaints against the police, but the powers of police authorities remained basically unchanged.
8. This Act (mainly) comes into force on 1 January 1986.
9. See chapter 4.
10. The Police (Grant) Order 1966 (s.1, 1966, No.223, as amended), made under s.31 of the Police Act 1964.
11. See chapter 3.
12. *Fisher* v. *Oldham Corporation* [1930] 2 KB 364.
13. *Ibid.*, pp.377-8, per McCardie J.
14. *Attorney General for New South Wales* v. *Perpetual Trustee Company (and others)* [1955] AC 457.
15. *Ibid.*, at pp.489-90.
16. *R* v. *Metropolitan Police Commissioner* ex parte *Blackburn* [1968] 2 QB 118; [1968] 1 All ER 763.
17. *Ibid.* [1968] 1 All ER 763, at p.769.
18. *R.* v. *Metropolitan Police Commissioner* ex parte *Blackburn and another* (No.3) [1973] 1 QB 241; [1973] 1 All ER 324.
19. *Ibid.* [1973] 1 All ER 324, as per Roskill LJ at p.338.
20. *Ibid.*, at p. 331.
21. Quoted in *R* v. *Chief Constable of Devon and Cornwall Constabulary* ex parte *Central Electricity Generating Board* [1981] 3 All ER 826, at p.831.
22. *Ibid.*
23. *Ibid.*, at p.833.

CHAPTER 3
The Police and Elected Representatives (2): Accountability in Practice

Police Authorities

If police authorities cannot tell their chief constables how to enforce the law, how meaningful are the powers which they do have — and what do they do with them?

Very little is known about the way in which police authorities operate and the extent of their influence over their force. Significantly, they rarely earn a mention in textbooks on policing, and the little material which is available shows that the majority of authorities play a very low-key role. This, it appears, is partly because of their limited powers but also because of a lack of political will on behalf of most authority members to exercise any influence over policing policies or practices.

Finance

The police authority's control over the budget potentially provides it with considerable influence over the distribution of resources, and hence policing methods and priorities. During periods of local government cuts, some authorities have indeed cut their police budget and questioned their force's spending priorities.[1] However, a considerable proportion of the expenditure is predetermined by the Home Secretary, principally police salaries, and the Home Office may also provide forces with some of their equipment, thus effectively bypassing the local decision-making process.

The authority's power over the budget is perhaps most seriously undermined by the Home Secretary's power to withhold the 50 per cent of the Authority's income which comes from central government, if he does not think the force is 'efficient'. This apparently is used as a threat periodically to make a police force or its authority conform to Home Office thinking on a particular issue.

The authorities necessarily delegate spending powers to their chief constable, giving him considerable discretion over how he chooses to spend money. When it was revealed by *The Observer* in September 1981, for example, that Greater Manchester force had purchased two sub-machine guns without even the knowledge of the police authority, the chair of the authority supported their right to have done so.[2] With a few exceptions, this willingness to allow chief constables to decide how much money they need and what to spend it on appears to be the normal practice.

It is clear, for example, from a journalist's account of a meeting of the Thames Valley Authority in 1980, at which the chief constable, Peter Imbert, called for a substantial increase in expenditure, that neither the chair nor the majority of members thought it appropriate to question his recommendation. Mr Imbert told them that he needed 750 more officers at a cost of £7.5 million and the authority readily agreed. Martin Kettle records:

> The members were obviously quite happy with the decision and the way it was reached . . . perhaps you wouldn't expect such a predominantly Conservative part of the country to cavil at new levels. But whether by design or accident, the meeting ended up by granting wide discretionary powers to the chairman and to the chief constable over an item involving a possible 16 per cent rise in expenditure and with wide policing implications.[3]

Moreover, Kettle points out, the item was not even on the agenda for the authority meeting: 'It is hard to avoid concluding that most members neither know nor care much about controlling what is happening'.[4]

In relation to technical issues, such as computerisation, Mike Brogden, who has studied the work of police authorities, thinks there is another explanation:

> Now in practice the lay member of the police authority has very little understanding about these technical developments. Consequently, he now restricts the decision-making area to that aspect with which he is most familiar, problems of police housing and the like. He, in a sense, abdicates any degree of decision-making with regard to the technical nature of police work.[5]

In one police authority which Brogden studied in 1976, the chief constable's office drew up the agenda for authority meetings and, he says, effectively exercised control over which issues came up for discussion and pre-empted the decision-making process:

> The members of the committee are inundated (the agenda is 2" thick) with data of a largely insignificant nature. Any disposition to be critical is lost in a morass of such detail. Peripheral issues are magnified as the basis of detailed analysis and discussion. Financial matters are minimised. The detail contributes to an image of the force as a painstaking body of experts. It implies that all issues have already been considered in depth. The nature of the tabulation provides a framework for their analysis which precludes the consideration of alternative factors.[6]

A typical example of this authority's attitude to its chief constable was its approach to his draft budget and his request for more officers. Although the authority had considerable room for manoeuvre in deciding the size of the establishment (number of officers) and hence in altering the cost, members of the authority believed that the chief constable based his assessment of the establishment that was necessary on objective criteria with which they could not argue. As one member put it: 'The chief constable never needs to justify his resources . . . all the figures are there . . . we are laymen. We can't quarrel with figures'.[7]

This account tallies with that of a meeting of the West Mercia Authority in 1979, which reportedly 'took less than a minute to approve an all time record level of spending for the next financial year'.[8]

The greatest ever controversy over responsibility for police spending arose in 1984 during the miners' industrial dispute. Conflict, between some Labour-controlled authorities on the one hand and the Home Secretary and chief constables on the other, arose partly out of the authorities' concern over the extent to which the burden of the dispute was falling on their ratepayers, and partly out of their concern that they had no control over the use to which the money was being put. Authorities in some of the areas directly affected by the dispute complained that their influence over their chief constable had been undermined by his receiving his instructions from the centralised National Reporting Centre at Scotland Yard; while some authorities in areas not directly affected complained that their chief constable was deciding how many officers to send to the mining areas in 'mutual aid', leaving the authority to pick up the bill. In some areas Labour and opposition councillors and their chief constable were united in arguing that the immense cost of policing the dispute could not be found within the police budget and that central government should bear the whole expense.

Pressure from the authorities led the Home Secretary to make a series of concessions gradually increasing the contribution the Treasury would make. This failed to satisfy many of the authorities still left to find savings of thousands of pounds in a police budget many months into the year. Nor did it resolve grey areas in the law highlighted by the dispute, in particular this question: is the authority's control over the budget absolute or can the chief constable insist on more money if he believes it necessary, in the circumstances, to enforce the law? Does the chief constable decide when his force is 'adequate and efficient' (and thus sufficiently funded) or the police authority?[9]

Reports from chief constables

It is the authorities' power to demand reports from their chief constable which brings them nearest to the arena of policy-making, and can provide a forum for discussing issues of local concern. Yet the chief constable's right to refuse to give a report (if it would not be in the 'public interest' or is not needed 'for the discharge of the functions of the police authority') severely limits the authorities' power in this respect.

There are few reported instances of chief constables refusing to submit such a report, however, and it is not clear how the Home Secretary would define 'public interest' or the 'authorities' functions' if asked to arbitrate. On the only occasion when a police authority did ask the Home Secretary to overrule its chief constable's refusal to submit a report, he refused to do so.[10] One legal commentator has interpreted the Act to mean that chief constables are not obliged to report on policy or law enforcement because '. . . it is not necessary for the discharge of the Authority's functions that he should provide information concerning particular matters of policy or law enforcement since these are not matters within the authority's jurisdiction'.[11]

Yet the House of Commons was told, during the passage of the Police Bill, that the matters police authorities would be able to ask for reports on *would* include 'the state of crime, the extent of police protection in a particular district, how the force is disposed between crime and traffic and other duties', and 'particular incidents which have given rise to complaints. In addition, the police authority will have a duty to inform itself that complaints are properly dealt with . . .'[12]

When an MP asked during the debate whether, for instance, a police authority would be able to call for a report on the use by the chief constable of mounted police to restore order, the Home Secretary replied, 'Unquestionably, the police authority could ask for a report . . . and could discuss it with him'.

MP: 'But he could refuse to give it'.

Home Secretary: '. . . in a case like that I can see no reason why the chief constable should not supply a report on request'.[13]

The Home Secretary continued by emphasising that the police authority 'will have every right to discuss with its chief constable how the men and equipment with which it has provided him can be most effectively used in conducting police operations. If, unhappily, the discussion resulted in such persistent disagreement between a police authority and its chief constable that the efficiency of the force seemed in question . . . then it would be the duty of the authority to set in motion machinery for requiring the chief constable to retire, subject to the Home Secretary's approval'.[14]

More recently a Home Secretary has confirmed:

> . . . the Police Act in no way inhibits discussion of operational issues between the chief constable and his police authority whether in the context of a review of resources necessary or more generally. The chief constable is generally accountable to his police authority for his policy.[15]

Nevertheless, the Chief Constable of Greater Manchester, for example, refused to provide his authority with the information it requested about the ten-day police operation at the Laurence Scott factory in February 1982. Mr Anderton said that it would not be in the public interest for him to disclose how many officers were deployed, at what cost, and from which areas they were withdrawn. The authority withdrew the question and replaced it with a question requiring less specific answers. When Mr Anderton submitted his report in March, the majority of the committee criticised the operation as misguided, damaging to police-community relations, and wasteful of public money. Mr Anderton answered that he had 'not come here to apologise', and said the level of policing required was his decision and not that of the authority.[16] Similarly, to take an example from Northern Ireland, the RUC chief constable refused to inform his authority about the handling of a complaint by James Rafferty, who was beaten up by police officers during his interrogation, on the grounds that the information 'was not necessary to the authority in order to discharge its functions'.[17]

Even if the authority gets the report, however, as it has no powers to instruct its chief constable, it cannot make him change any of the policies or practices which it describes. As a dissenting member of the Royal Commission recognised:

> These reports will, however, be of little practical value unless the police authorities or the Home Secretary are given the power to do something about them . . . This novel method of government through reports, without power to do anything, is a new development in the science of politics.[18]

This was indeed Merseyside Police Authority's experience when it found itself dissatisfied with the report it received from its chief constable after the 1981 riots.[19]

As with finance, however, it appears that many authorities have actually chosen not to exercise even the limited powers they do have. A unique survey of police authorities conducted by the Association of Metropolitan Authorities (AMA) and Association of County Councils (ACC) during 1976 revealed that, although a majority of chief constables reported to their authority regularly on the policing of their area, in ten out of the forty-one authorities covered (London's forces do not appear to have been included) this was not the case. Similarly, although most authorities used their power to *request* specific reports, seven did not do so and in only ten cases was it a frequent occurrence. One (rural) authority *never* requested information on policing and did not receive regular reports.[20]

In thirty-one out of forty-one authorities, guidance on local problems was given to the chief constable but, according to the survey, only on a very narrow basis and on limited issues such as the siting of police stations or car parks. The major activity, it says, was the raising of 'constituency' problems by individual members. Only nineteen out of the forty-one authorities claimed to contribute formally to the solution of social problems, although the questionnaire had given examples of 'a fair cross section of issues of acute concern to the community'.

Even in those authorities which regularly receive reports, it may actually be the chief constable who is taking the initiative and choosing to provide the information. 'I endeavour to pre-empt things', the Chief Constable of Thames Valley told Kettle in 1980. 'I pick up these apprehensions through the press . . . through the people who write to me, and I take it upon myself to tell the police authority'. He had just decided to give his authority an overview of the controversial Thames Valley computer experiment because 'the public has got to know that we have on there records of people who are not convicted of crimes. They have got to know why we've got them, and then they've got to tell me whether or not we can carry on keeping them'.

Yet the timing of his decision was such that the experiment was already completed and evaluated by the Home Office before the police authority received this information. As Kettle concluded: 'the decision comes first, and the debate to provide it with public legitimation comes afterwards'.[21]

The way in which the Cleveland force came to set up its version of a special patrol group illustrates the same pattern of behaviour. NCCL's Northumberland and Durham group heard in August 1980 that the force had set up a 'Special Operations Service' and wrote to the chair of the authority to ask whether his committee had discussed this development before the decision was taken and why such a task force was felt to be necessary in Cleveland.

The chairperson's reply was not informative: 'Such a development is, as you know, a matter for the chief constable as is the appreciation of the policing problems within the county'. He did not say whether or not the authority had been consulted about the formation of the new unit. NCCL then directed the same questions to the chief constable, whose assistant replied: 'The chief constable is not prepared to supply the information you require'. But he did say that the police authority had discussed the matter — two weeks *after* the chairperson had replied to NCCL's enquiry, on 19 September. The minutes of that meeting record that the chief constable submitted a report which stated baldly that: 'As part of the re-organisation of the force a Special Operations Service was formed on 4 August 1980'. It informed the authority as to how many officers were in the squad and the kind of operations on which they were deployed, including 'saturation policing'. The report, according to the minutes, was simply 'noted'.[22]

Although not required by law to do so (unless requested by the authority), some chief constables provide their authority with regular reports during the year, Sussex's chief constable, for example, tabling a report for each quarterly meeting. His report to the first meeting in 1984 included an analysis of recent crime statistics, an account of the policing of recent demonstrations by animal rights sympathisers, an estimate of the cost of implementing the new Police and Criminal Evidence Bill, an expression of concern about the detention of prisoners in police cells, and details of personnel changes.

Appointment of senior officers

The authority's responsibility for appointing senior officers clearly accords it some distinct influence over the policy and direction of the force, but even here its scope for choice is severely curtailed by the Home Secretary's power to veto its choice. Not only does the Home Office indicate on the shortlist which applicants it would be prepared to endorse, but it has on at least one occasion threatened to withdraw its 50 per cent grant to a force if the authority did not accept its choice.[23] Moreover, the Home Secretary is known to have used his power in relation to the selection process in order to influence one authority on an entirely unrelated decision.

When the post of chief constable fell vacant in Durham in 1981, the police authority duly forwarded its shortlist of six names to the Home Office. But the Home Secretary refused to approve the list until Durham, and the neighbouring Cleveland force, agreed to reconsider a Home Office proposal that the two forces should merge, a proposal that both forces had already rejected. In the event the authorities again refused to merge and the shortlist was returned to Durham, now reduced to four names.

When Durham authority subsequently met to interview the candidates, according to a member of the authority, a most unusual interviewing procedure was adopted by the chairman which actually prevented the members of the authority questioning the candidates freely. Each candidate was given one written question five minutes before he met the committee; his 'interview' then consisted of his answering this one question. Authority members were not allowed follow-up questions in order 'to avoid any favouritism, by people feeding questions to their favourite candidate'. They were then asked to vote once, the candidate who received the most votes being appointed.[24]

When the Chief Constable of Sussex retired in 1983 the intervention of the Home Secretary in the appointment of his successor aroused the anger of the Conservative and opposition councillors alike. The Labour and Liberal councillors apparently did not protest, however, over the way in which the appointments committee was chosen. The councillors and magistrates who formed the appointments committee were nominated not by the authority itself (which was not consulted about the composition of the committee) but by the chairman. From the (joint) authority he chose four Conservatives, one Labour, one Liberal and one magistrate, reflecting the political balance in the authority.

This panel met and drew up a shortlist of candidates, relying on their own assessment of the kind of chief constable Sussex needed, as the authority had held no discussion on the qualities or qualifications they should look for. The shortlist selected included chief constables of smaller forces and some deputy chief constables. The list was subsequently sent to the Home Office for its approval. To the annoyance of the panel the Home Office replied that it was not prepared to ratify any applicants who were currently only deputy chief constables and removed their names from the shortlist. The panel strongly resented what it saw as Home Office interference in local decision-making and the chairman wrote to the Home Secretary criticising the interference in strong terms.

Of the three remaining candidates on the shortlist, two more were interviewed (one having withdrawn). In contrast to the procedure adopted in Durham, the appointments panel were all permitted to ask questions. A member of the Inspectorate was also present. The panel decided to appoint Roger Birch, then Chief Constable of Warwickshire, who was invited to the next meeting of the authority at which his appointment was duly ratified.[25]

If the authority's power to appoint senior officers cannot be said to accord it a significant influence over the force, nor can its power to dismiss senior officers be considered a realistic means of calling them to account for their actions. It is an action to be taken in the last resort which could not, and was not intended to, give it any influence over the day-to-day operation of the force.

Complaints against the police

Although the police authority is responsible for checking the way in which complaints against the police are dealt with, once again it is given no powers with which to fulfil this responsibility effectively. The practice in some authorities is for a subcommittee to arrive early for each authority meeting to inspect the register of complaints received. This file contains only the bare outlines of the facts, and members of the committee are not allowed to see the investigating officers' files. During the passage of the 1964 Act the Home Secretary said that it would be open to the authority to call for a report from its chief constable on the manner in which a particular complaint had been handled,[26] but the refusal of Merseyside's chief constable to report to his authority on the investigation into the death of Jimmy Kelly, and that of the chief constable of the RUC in the Rafferty case, would suggest that they can refuse to do so with impunity.

The AMA/ACC survey revealed very little information about the authorities' practices in relation to complaints other than to confirm that they did 'examine the records', some having a subcommittee to undertake this task, others operating a rota of all members. Significantly, 'there was little support for the suggestion that members should be able to ask for a particular complaints file, as it was felt that examination of a few files taken at random' (selected by the police?) 'would be adequate for the purpose'.

Public relations and the press

Although police authorities claimed, in their replies to the AMA/ACC survey, that they had made 'arrangements' for fostering good relations between the police and the public, it was clear in eight cases that no arrangements had been made at all, and the remaining thirty-three authorities could in fact cite few examples. The survey concluded that, in some cases, the examples were not so much of police authorities' involvement in activities as 'the absence of discouragement of activities of the chief constable to whom the whole of the intitiative was left'.

Although one authority allowed members of the press to remain throughout the whole meeting, the majority excluded the press for some items of business and one authority would not allow the press in at all. The survey found that, as regards briefing the press, 'the chief constable and/or press officer is far more involved than the chairman'.

When NCCL's Sussex group discovered in 1981 that the public was excluded from Sussex Police Authority meetings it conducted a survey to find out which authorities allowed public access and which did not. It found that, although twenty-nine of those which replied were open to the public, not all of them regarded this as a public right. The combined authorities were the most secretive and closed. Although the public have a qualified right of access to *local authority* meetings, Sussex claimed that, as one of the ten combined authorities, it was a 'body corporate' and not a local authority; hence it did not have to allow the public in.

A closer reading of the law enabled the group to point out that under the 1972 Local Government Act, police authorities *are* defined as local authorities and Sussex has since allowed public access. Fourteen authorities failed to reply to the survey and four refused to co-operate — Devon and Cornwall refusing because it 'did not see the issue as being of importance'.[27] NCCL's Somerset group was told by Avon and Somerset authority that the public were denied access because 'the room at King's Weston House is unfortunately rather small to accommodate more than the actual members of the committee' and 'parking facilities are totally inadequate at other possible venues'. Undeterred, a group member did attend the meeting, 'squeezing into a corner seat'.[28]

Relationship with chief constables

The AMA/ACC survey and subsequent seminar revealed that the majority of authorities at that time adopted a deferential role to their chief constables and, not surprisingly, reported that their relationships with them were 'generally satisfactory, it being recognised that the chief constable had absolute responsibility for operational matters . . .'.

The main points of common agreement between authority representatives who met to discuss the issue early in 1977 were the need for 'full support for the police forces doing a good job under very difficult circumstances', 'the need for a firm and open partnership' between the Home Office, police authorities and the police, and 'the importance of good and sensitive public relations'. It is clear from the proceedings that the authorities saw their role primarily as representing the police to the public rather than representing the public to the police.[29] Kettle's article on the Thames Valley Authority supports this account. The Conservative chairman told him, 'It's the job of the authority to provide the tools to do the job. It's my job', he added, 'to go to our chaps and say "Well done".'[30]

One member of an authority which Brogden studied at this time, contrasting the police authority with other local government committees of which he was a member, told him: 'We would often over-ride what the chief fire officer wanted. We would never do that with the chief constable.'[31]

Brogden found that the party political clashes that were evident on the other local government committees at the time were 'completely absent' from the police authority, and the eighteen members of the authority whom he interviewed were adamant that 'politics never intruded here'. Some concern was expressed at the AMA/ACC seminar that individual members of the authorities had very little involvement in police affairs, and in some instances were 'little more than rubber stamping decisions already made', and Kettle found that it was in fact only the chairperson who had regular contact with the chief constable, spending 'about an hour a week' talking to him on the telephone and attending police functions. It was also the chairperson who, with the chief constable, had taken on the task of lobbying the Home Office for the increase in funds he wanted.

Mr Whitelaw, when Home Secretary, endorsed this picture of chairmen identifying closely with the chief constable:

> . . . I see the chairman of the police authority, I admit I don't see the whole police authority, but when I see the chairman, he frequently spends a great deal of his time, and I very much welcome this, trying to persuade me — often I don't need to be persuaded — what a good chief constable he has.[32]

Role of magistrates

Little evidence is available about the role which the non-elected magistrates actually play on police authorities. Although, under the 1964 Act, they must constitute one third of the committee, their presence has led some county councils to depart from the normal local government practice of allocating the committee seats between the political parties according to their numbers on the council. When Merseyside County Council was under Conservative control between 1977 and 1981, for example, the twenty 'political' seats on the authority were apportioned between the three political parties in accordance with their respective strength on the council. The result, according to the leader of the Conservative group, was that '. . . had the minority Labour and Liberal parties wished to vote with the magistrates against the controlling Conservatives we could have been outvoted — and indeed on one occasion we were'.[33]

When a Labour administration subsequently took over, however, it treated the magistrates as part of the opposition when allocating seats, a practice which the chairperson of the committee, Margaret Simey, believes is 'common throughout the country'. She says: 'Police authorities have, in fact, little choice in the matter. If the leading party is to exercise its responsibilities it is essential that it retains a majority over the opposition and magistrates combined'.[34]

The difference in approach is based on a conflicting view of the role of the magistrates. While the Conservative leader believes police authorities have 'two thirds of their members political and one third magistrates', Margaret Simey says that the magistrates *are* political *and* tend to vote with the Conservatives. One reason why the magistrates can become quite a powerful block on the authority is that they do not change at each election. One magistrate member of West Midlands Authority told the author in 1982 that he had been a member of the authority since it was set up in 1964 — and on the watch committee before that!

NCCL had direct experience of magistrates' voting power when it wrote to each authority in January 1982 asking them to call for a report from their chief constable on the safeguards operated by his force (a) to prevent inaccurate or irrelevant data being kept on police records, and (b) to ensure that no unauthorised access to the information took place. At the next meeting of the Cleveland Authority, a motion supporting our proposal was defeated when the non-elected magistrate members joined with Conservatives and Independents to reject it.[35]

Powers of the Local Council

As the powers of the police authority are derived directly from statute the council cannot, in most cases, control directly the way in which it uses these powers. However, there are a number of ways in which councillors who are not on the authority can exercise some influence. First, they appoint two thirds of the membership of the authority. Secondly, they can question a representative of the authority (usually the chairperson) during meetings of the full council, and finally, except in the case of combined authorities, they have the final say over the police budget. In practice, councillors in the majority party can exert most influence over the authority through 'group' meetings, that is the regular meetings of councillors in the same party, usually held shortly before the meetings of the council. While meetings of Conservative and Labour groups in many areas rarely discuss police authority business, in other areas authority business is regularly discussed at Labour group meetings and the chairpersons of those authorities consider themselves as accountable to the group as any other local government chairperson. Policy suggestions on both financial and wider policing matters may originate in group discussions as did, for example, the policy of Nottinghamshire Police Authority not to purchase plastic bullets for its force.[36]

In contrast, the AMA/ACC survey in 1976 found that four authorities never reported to the full council and a further two did not report regularly. Moreover, the councillors' statutory right to ask questions is frequently further curtailed. The authority has no statutory obligation to present its minutes to council, although the ability of councillors to raise questions about its work is clearly limited if it does not. In only eleven out of thirty-one county authorities were the full authority minutes submitted, and in many cases it was specifically stated that this was for information only; in other cases, reports or extracts from the minutes were selective, usually relating to items of expenditure where specific county council approval was required.[37]

In Merseyside, it was found that the clerk to the authority used to indicate items on the authority's minutes, such as specific complaints, which were 'for information only', a ruling which, for example, prevented councillors discussing the investigation into Jimmy Kelly's death, at a council meeting in October 1979.[38] West Sussex County Council receives only a 'brief report' of the authority's meeting, members of the authority having no say in the content of that report, according to one member of the authority.[39] It also receives the chief constable's quarterly reports to the authority. Councillors occasionally ask questions but no debate is allowed and members of the authority are not permitted to supplement the chairman's replies. Moreover, while both the authority and the council meet quarterly, the meetings are often out of step so that reports from the authority to the council can be long out of date.

Powers of the Home Secretary

If police authorities' powers are more apparent than real, this position is reversed in the case of the Home Secretary and his department. Although the Home Secretary and Home Office consistently keep a low profile as regards their involvement in policing, their influence is undoubtedly far greater than that of police authorities. Yet Home Secretaries will only answer questions from MPs on those areas for which they have direct ministerial responsibility, and their decisions, for example regarding regulations on equipment, do not require a positive vote by Parliament before coming into force.

Accountability to Parliament

The constitutional position regarding the extent of an MP's right to obtain information about the policing of his/her constituency through the Home Secretary is not at all clear. The Home Secretary's power to call for reports from chief constables suggests that they are answerable to Parliament through the Home Secretary. However, although Home Secretaries answer parliamentary questions relating to provincial forces on administrative matters, or regarding whether a report is to be called for, they have

> shown a marked reluctance to answer parliamentary questions on police and law enforcement matters relating to forces other than the Metropolitan Police . . . The result is that Members of Parliament representing constituencies outside London cannot successfully ask parliamentary questions on matters relating to their local force which they could successfully ask if the force was the Metropolitan Police.[40]

The obverse of this situation, however, is that, while provincial police authorities do make regular reports to their county council, the Home Secretary does not report to Parliament after his meetings with the Metropolitan Commissioner. It must also be said that even London MPs are not always successful in extracting information about the Metropolitan Police from the Home Secretary. He not infrequently refuses to provide the information, claiming that it is an 'operational matter' and hence under the Commissioner's jurisdiction. In July 1979, for example, when Jo Richardson MP asked whether it was common practice for the police in London to collect details of the organisations and speakers at political meetings, whether the Home Secretary endorsed such a practice and if so on what basis, and if he would say in what form the information was collected, and so on, Mr Whitelaw's answer on this highly controversial police practice was simply: 'These are operational matters for the Commissioner. I fully support his collecting information necessary for discharging his responsibility for the maintenance of public order'.[41]

The answers relating to provincial forces are often equally unhelpful. When Bob Cryer MP asked, for example, whether the Home Secretary 'will institute an investigation into the methods of detection used by provincial police forces, with a view to establishing the best procedures available', he was told: 'The methods used in detecting crime are a matter for Chief Officers of Police. We are sure that all Chief Officers are concerned that the methods used by their officers should be the best available'.[42]

When Stanley Cohen MP asked what administrative co-ordination existed between forces to help enforce the law on illegal possession of firearms, where offences have been committed by nationally organised extremist groups, he received no information at all. All he was told was: 'To ensure the proper investigation of alleged crime, Chief Officers of Police maintain the closest co-ordination between forces'.[43] And when Mr Dafydd Wigley MP asked the Home Secretary what guidance is issued to the police as to the use of short-barrel 12-bore shotguns he was simply told: 'It would not be in the interests of police effectiveness to make public the guidance that has been given to Chief Officers of Police about the use of specific weapons, including shotguns'.[44]

When the Home Secretary does agree to call for a report from a chief constable, it appears that he relies on the police to cover all the relevant information. Yet on two recent occasions the press has found that information he subsequently passed on to Parliament was inaccurate.

On the basis of Merseyside chief constable Ken Oxford's report on the use of CS gas against individuals involved in disturbances in Toxteth, the Home Secretary told the House of Commons that 'in no instance were any such weapons aimed directly at individuals'.[45] However, from subsequent ballistic evidence available to the Home Office, which indicated that a number of cartridges were fired directly at people, from police statements given to the Home Office-initiated internal police enquiry (which the *New Statesman* obtained), and from evidence which emerged at subsequent court hearings, the *New Statesman* concluded that Oxford 'had failed to seek relevant ballistic opinion on what had occurred', and that his report 'misled and misinformed the Home Secretary, who in turn misinformed Parliament'. The *New Statesman* challenged the Home Secretary to take action as a result of the findings, 'if police accountability is to have any meaning'. No action was taken.[46]

In January 1983, *The Observer* revealed that the Home Secretary had wrongly informed the House of Commons about the number of times London's police had used guns in a given period, underestimating both the number of incidents when the police used guns and the number of people they had shot and wounded. Scotland Yard told *The Observer* that 'the use of guns is monitored closely' but admitted that reports on two of the cases traced by *The Observer* appeared to be missing.[47]

The Home Secretary's power to order an enquiry under the 1964 Police Act has been used only very rarely: to investigate the Challoner affair in 1965[48] and the Red Lion Square demonstration in 1975 in which Kevin Gately died,[49] and to set up the Scarman Enquiry into the disturbances in Brixton in 1981.[50]

The Home Secretary can also order an extra-statutory enquiry such as the Fisher enquiry into the Confait case,[51] which investigated the interrogation and prosecution of three South London youths for the murder of Maxwell Confait. Sir Henry Fisher's criticisms of the treatment of the youths (who were subsequently proved to be innocent and awarded record compensation) led to the establishment of the Royal Commission on Criminal Procedure in 1978.

Such enquiries can, as the Scarman Enquiry showed, investigate and draw attention to policing policies and practices, but only, necessarily, after something has gone seriously wrong. Moreover, the Home Secretary is not obliged to order an enquiry however serious the incident. Merlyn Rees, Labour Home Secretary in 1979, came under considerable pressure to set up an enquiry into the police handling of the anti-National Front demonstration in Southall on 23 April, during which a police officer killed a school teacher, Blair Peach. He refused, as did his Conservative successor, elected two weeks later.

The Home Secretary who introduced the 1964 Police Act said then of the power to set up an enquiry: 'I trust that this will be a weapon of last resort, but if I am not satisfied that all the truth has come out, I shall not hesitate to use it'.[52]

It cannot be said that his successors have adopted this principle.

The Inspectorate

The Home Secretary may also order a special inspection of any force by the Inspectorate of Constabulary (HMI), such as that into the City of Leeds police in 1971-2, the report of which was never published.

The Inspectorate is closely involved in the Home Office's policy-making process, drawing on its members' experience as former police officers and its annual inspection of all provincial police forces. Significantly, the Inspectorate reports direct to the Home Office and not to police authorities, which are apparently not even permitted to see the report on their force. Its inspection findings are a closely guarded secret, only the Chief Inspector's Report being published. This is notably uninformative about the work of the HMI itself (this aspect covering some one or two pages), the report providing only a summary of information about police manpower, resources, training, crime, policing methods and equipment, and complaints.

In recent years each such report has stated that most, if not all, the provincial and City of London forces have been inspected and that 'No shortcomings were found which would prejudice a police authority's claim to Exchequer grant on approved expenditure'. Sometimes it adds: 'The measures which were thought necessary to rectify any shortcomings revealed in the course of inspections were brought about by suggestion and discussion with Chief Officers in the course of inspection visits', but there is no indication of what these shortcomings might be.

The HMI regularly participates in Home Office working parties or study groups, such as the review of police arrangements for handling spontaneous public disorder after the St. Paul's disturbances in Bristol in April 1980 and the Working Group on Protective Clothing and Equipment after the Brixton disturbances the following year. The Inspectorate is also involved in the controversial unit for co-ordinating mutual aid at Scotland Yard, the National Reporting Centre, which is directed by the President of the Association of Chief Police Officers (ACPO).[53] It was a member of the Inspectorate who led the review of West Yorkshire Police's investigation in the case of the 'Yorkshire Ripper', despite protests from Yorkshire MPs that a review by an Inspector who had himself worked in the West Yorkshire force would be 'a total police whitewash'.[54] The review resulted from public concern that it had taken the police five and a half years to establish that Peter Sutcliffe was responsible for the murders, despite the fact that he had been interviewed by them on nine separate occasions.

The 1980 HMI Report states, characteristically without

explanation, that the Inspectorate was reorganised during the year and the Inspectors allocated 'specific functional responsibilities so as to ensure their closer participation in the advisory and policy making processes of the Home Office'; while the 1981 Report adds that, as a consequence of these arrangements, considerable demands are made on the HMI's time, 'which may in some instances result in some adjustment to the scope and extent of force inspections'.

Finance and support services

The Home Secretary's most important powers are, perhaps, those about which least is known, including his control over the Exchequer grant, which has 'provided a basis for the part played by the Home Office in securing the introduction of more efficient methods of policing'.[55] In 1947, for example, the Home Secretary threatened to withhold £100,000 from the Exchequer's grant to Salford Watch Committee when he refused to approve of its choice of the deputy as chief constable in order to secure the appointment of the man of his choice.[56]

The Home Office also acts as a research centre and think-tank on new policing methods and techniques and may ask individual forces to experiment with a new technique before recommending its use nationwide. Unit beat policing began, for example, as a Home Office experiment in Accrington and was later adopted throughout the country. The Home Office cannot, as we have seen, impose new methods on chief constables, but it does have regular discussions with them prior to issuing circulars recommending a shift in priorities or a new course of action — for example, that issued in June 1982 calling for the establishment of liaison committees with the public, a circular which, because it sought community involvement, was, exceptionally, made public.[57] Although the wording of such circulars may be didactic — a recent circular on the Prevention of Terrorism Act, for instance, tells chief constables that a particular arrest power, defined very widely in the statute, 'should' only be used in certain limited circumstances — they are in theory only advisory. The wording does however suggest that chief constables are expected to act as 'advised'. As the circulars are rarely made public it is impossible to estimate the extent to which they do so.

Computerised command and control systems were introduced after the Home Office's Police Scientific Development Branch set up an experiment in the Birmingham force in 1972, followed by the testing of a more sophisticated system in Glasgow in 1973.[58] Later that year the Home Office sent a memorandum to all chief constables explaining the potential of such systems to police forces which have since placed their orders.

Experiments of this kind are not initiated by the Home Office without consultation. Two bodies play a major role in influencing its policy: the Association of Chief Police Officers (ACPO) and HMI Constabulary. Although ACPO began as a staff association for senior officers it is now an influential pressure group, staffed by its own secretariat based at Scotland Yard, and has 'developed for itself a central role in government policy assessment and planning'.[59]

ACPO's views are most apparent when it is lobbying publicly for changes in the law, for example in its evidence to the Royal Commission on Criminal Procedure. But it also has a series of subcommittees such as its Computer Development Committee, which meets privately with the Home Office. The 1979 HMI Report notes, for example, in relation to the developing use of computers by police forces, that: 'I am glad to see that the Home Office and the Association of Chief Police Officers are jointly working towards the establishment of standards which forces will be able to use in procuring computer systems'.[60]

Thames Valley's controversial experiment with computerising the police officer's 'notebook', recording local gossip as well as factual information, was also initiated and paid for by the Home Office. But Thames Valley's chief constable, Peter Imbert, did not agree to the experiment without first discussing it with his ACPO colleagues on the Computer Development Committee:

> We canvass this sort of thing among ourselves. We make a recommendation to the ACPO Council and then ACPO Council will decide, and that's every Chief Constable. If they accept the recommendations, then we'll adopt it. If they don't, even though I think it's a damn good idea, I don't adopt it.[61]

Secrecy

The Home Office is consistently secretive about its involvement in policing matters such as, for instance, the nature of police computer facilities and the extent of the personal records held on them. In a Home Office booklet on the Police National Computer (PNC) in 1978, for example, the reproduction of a photograph of a chart showing the categories of persons who may be listed in the wanted/missing persons index was 'deliberately left unclear' according to a Home Office spokesman.[62]

In his description of police computer facilities, Duncan Campbell records that even MPs have found the Home Office unwilling to provide information about the PNC's facilities, either answering their questions disingenuously with technical data on the size of the computer's electronic store, or explaining in the most general terms that it is related to 'the prevention and detection of crime'.[63] On other occasions the answers have been simply misleading, as was the reply which began: 'Information about political beliefs and activities is not held on the Police National Computer', and continued, contradictorily, 'occasionally information about association with an organisation has been held for a limited period in the index of suspected and stolen vehicles when a police officer has judged it relevant when reporting a vehicle as suspected of being used in connection with crime'[64] — an unusually informative answer prompted only by the revelation in court that a PNC check had resulted in an officer being told that the owner of the vehicle he had stopped was 'a prominent member of the Anti-Blood Sports League'.[65]

The PNC also provides an illustration of the sort of method the Home Office uses to enable the police to obtain additional information without authorisation by Parliament. The PNC's Vehicle Owners Index contains a description of every vehicle in the country, obtained directly (and updated daily) from the Driver and Vehicle Licensing Centre in Swansea. Owners (and drivers) are legally obliged to inform the DVLC of any change of address (on penalty of a fine), so that in practice the PNC is informed of the change of address of every vehicle owner. As Campbell points out: 'Each owner, by a neat administrative trick, is now legally obliged to inform the police of any change of address. The merging of the two databanks created in effect a new law, without any discussion whatsoever in Parliament, let alone explicit statutory authority'.[66]

Campbell concludes his description of police computer facilities with the observation that:

> In no case has public discussion of police computers been full and frank; the official responses range from the stonewalling of a government committee by the Metropolitan Police, to dishonest and misleading answers in Parliament. In most cases, minimisation of public discussion has rested on the simple proposition that the public and its representatives are best kept in ignorance. This view is generally supported by arguments about security, or the difficulties arising from explaining complicated technology. Such views are elitist, arrogant and dishonest.[67]

A second example of the Home Office's unwillingness to encourage public discussion on policing matters and to concede a greater degree of accountability has been its attitude to the Special Branch.

It was not until 1978 that an MP, Robin Cook, managed to apply sufficient pressure to persuade a Home Secretary to reveal for the first time the number of police officers working in the Special Branch. But the Home Secretary still refused to answer the key question: who are the targets of their surveillance, and why? Nevertheless, his new spirit of openness appeared to influence chief constables, twenty-two of whom revealed for the first time in their annual reports that they *had* Special Branches (only Durham had previously admitted this), and prompted the HMI to explain the Special Branch's task as dealing 'mainly' with 'criminal offences against the security of the state, with terrorist or subversive organisations, with certain protection duties, with keeping watch on seaports and airports, and with making enquiries about aliens'.[68]

The key word was 'subversive', which Lord Denning had officially defined (in his 1963 report on the Profumo affair) as people who 'would contemplate the overthrow of government by *unlawful means*'. Yet, without explanation, the Home Secretary told Parliament in 1978 that subversive activities were now defined as those which 'threaten the safety or wellbeing of the state, and are intended to *undermine* or overthrow parliamentary democracy by *political*, *industrial* or *violent means*' (our emphasis)[69] — a definition which would appear to authorise Special Branch surveillance of individuals involved in lawful political and industrial activity. As Patricia Hewitt has argued:

> The uncertainty about how and when the definition became part of official policy underlines the crucial fact that a central element of constitutional law, the definition of the enemies of the state and therefore the identification of the legitimate targets of police surveillance, had been fundamentally changed not by Parliament, not even by the courts, but secretly by the security services, the police, civil servants and Ministers.[70]

An all-party group of MPs, the Home Affairs Select Committee, decided in 1984 to investigate the operation of the Special Branch during 1985. It remains to be seen, when its report is published, how much co-operation and information they have received from the Home Office and individual police forces.

The Example of Merseyside

A number of conflicts which have arisen between police authorities and their chief constables, and the role which the Home Secretary of the day has played in these conflicts, have highlighted the limits of police authorities' power to call chief constables to account and to influence their future policies and practices. The case of Merseyside Police Authority, however, an authority unique in the extent to which it has in recent years endeavoured to exert some influence over its chief constable, also demonstrates the steps which authorities can take, using the limited powers they possess.

Early in 1979, Margaret Simey, a Labour member of Merseyside Police Authority, had written in *Rights:*

> the Police Committee of today can only be likened to an Education Committee whose role has shrunk to nothing more than the provision of an 'adequate and efficient' teaching force over whose actual deployment they have absolutely no control...
>
> ... how does it come about that Police Committees are universally disregarded, and their members frequently complain of powerlessness and frustration? Even more important, what, if anything, can be done to revitalise an agency with so powerful a potential?[71]

In the event it was a series of serious allegations of police brutality in the Knowsley area of Liverpool, culminating in the death in police custody of Jimmy Kelly, that provided the catalyst.

Widespread concern about the police's 'get tough' policy and the mounting allegations of excessive violence had led Knowsley District Council to pass a motion of no confidence in the police, while the local MP, Sir Harold Wilson, called for a public enquiry into Kelly's death.

In a BBC *Panorama* investigation on 1 October 1979, Councillor Simey said that the police behaviour raised fundamental questions about the accountability of chief constables for their operational decisions; she believed that 'the police have taken over the whole field of political decisions and police committees generally have opted out of their responsibility'. Merseyside's chief constable, Ken Oxford, responded by dismissing the allegations, denying that any problem existed and rejecting the BBC's enquiries as 'impertinent and presumptuous'.[72] When he was asked at a meeting of the authority whether it was true that he had set up an enquiry, and if so by whom and into what, he refused 'with some passion'[73] to provide any further information over and above what he had given the press, and told the authority to 'keep out of my force's business'.[74] He later accused those councillors critical of his stance of 'vituperative and misinformed comment'.[75]

Mr Oxford had indeed called in David Gerty, assistant chief constable of the West Midlands force, to investigate Kelly's death, but the authority was never to see his report. Mr Oxford deflected all criticism by alleging that his critics had questionable political motives — a theme to be taken up later by his counterpart in Greater Manchester, James Anderton. Mr Oxford's attitude finally drew a response from the Conservative leader of the county council, who stated:

> At times he's arrogant . . . he talks of his police force. It isn't . . . it's our police force. Everyone's. Political direction of a police force or of a single policeman is unacceptable. Increasingly unacceptable is the distant authoritarianism of certain ego-inflated chief police officers . . . a small group of intriguers who shape public opinion.[76]

The death of Jimmy Kelly, coming in the wake of other deaths in custody, led MPs, in particular Michael Meacher, to ask the Home Secretary for information about the people who had died in custody. Mr Whitelaw proved as reluctant as Ken Oxford to provide this basic information. Details about the people who had died in police custody in the last ten years could, he replied, 'only be obtained at disproportionate cost'[77] — a decision he later reversed in response to public pressure.

Meanwhile, the DPP had decided that there was insufficient evidence to prosecute the officers who, according to five eyewitnesses, had kicked and punched Kelly during his arrest,[78] despite the fact that it was now known that Gerty, on whose report the DPP's decision was based, had failed to interview two witnesses. The Home Secretary rejected the demands for an independent enquiry under section 32 of the Police Act, insisting that the existing complaints procedure was adequate, although it was reported that he had apparently not even read Gerty's report when he made his decision.[79] No officers were disciplined as a result of the Kelly incident, and the Gerty report was never made public. Phil Scraton, in his study of the conflict, concludes that:

> . . . the greatest cause for concern is not that the chief constable abused his powers but that he used them legitimately. In real terms the police committee was shown to have no powers to make the chief constable accountable for what were most serious doubts over operational policy and practices.[80]

In May 1981 the Labour Party took control of Merseyside

County Council and Margaret Simey became chairperson of the authority. The Labour Party's manifesto had declared:

> . . . really energetic exercise of such powers as the authority already possesses could do much to restore the balance of power between police and elected members. Police authority meetings would become a forum at which police and elected members would discuss together, in public, ways and means of dealing with the dilemmas and difficulties of policing a modern community. The aim would be to produce an agreed policy, understood by the public and acceptable to them.[81]

By the time the civil disturbances erupted in Liverpool in June 1981, the police authority had been under Labour control for some two months. The methods the chief constable adopted to disperse the crowds, including the firing of seventy-four CS gas canisters and driving police vehicles at speed into the crowd, were highly contentious, yet Mr Oxford failed even to contact the new chairperson to discuss what was happening. The CS gas was fired at people in the streets (for the first time ever in Great Britain) despite manufacturers' instructions that the kind of canisters stocked by the police should not be used to disperse crowds *and* Home Office guidelines that CS gas was 'for use in dealing with armed criminals or violently insane persons in buildings from which they cannot be dislodged without danger or loss of life. The tear smoke *would not be used in any other circumstances*' (our emphasis).[82] Far from calling Mr Oxford to account for his total disregard of these instructions, Mr Whitelaw told Parliament the following day that his decision was 'totally right'.

Meanwhile, the police authority was left to complain about Mr Oxford's behaviour while being powerless to do anything effective about it. When it criticised him for spending £53,000 on riot control equipment without permission he retorted: 'It's a matter of interpretation. There is an escape clause in the rule book that in exceptional circumstances a chief officer can make a value judgement and tell people afterwards'.[83] When Mr Oxford brought in an outside officer to investigate the death of David Moore, killed during the riots by a police vehicle, but not to investigate the case of Paul Conroy who suffered a broken back in similar circumstances, the authority found itself powerless to alter his decision.

When the authority finally received a written report from Mr Oxford in September it refused to approve it, complaining that it was almost entirely a chronological account of what had happened and not an explanation of police tactics. Councillor Simey said later that calling for reports was simply not effective as a weapon of accountability: 'We have no effective weapon to bring chief constables to account . . . we are left to decide whether the police can buy a second-hand horsebox to take horses to football matches'.[84]

The approach which the authority later took to a proposal from its chief constable to extend the force's computer facilities marked a significant departure from the role normally adopted by police authorities faced with such a proposal.

Merseyside force already had a £2 million command and control computer and wanted to purchase a second computer, at a cost of £1.8 million, to store criminal intelligence and details of reported crimes and criminal records, thus making the information more rapidly and widely available to officers on the beat.

At its meeting on 29 June 1982, the authority asked its chief constable to draw up a code of conduct for the use of the new system before it would agree to purchase it. It also asked him to give the authority a report covering all previous computer proposals and possible future developments, and decided to organise a seminar to help authority members consider the influence of computerised record systems on policing techniques.

The chief constable agreed to prepare a code of conduct which, with a number of mutually agreed modifications, was accepted by the authority at a subsequent meeting in November. The code covers the first step in the introduction of the new computer system, the computerisation of information now held on manual records, and includes among its safeguards that:

- Only factual records, not criminal intelligence, should be included.
- Regular checks should be made to ensure the accuracy of the conversion from manual records to the computer.
- Access to printed copies should be restricted and all printed output shredded as soon as possible.
- Access to the computer should be controlled, with daily checks on who has used it, and on information that has been added.

The chairman of the authority's computer panel (a subcommittee) said that, before they moved on to the next stage of the project — the criminal records computer system:

> I should imagine that we would be looking for modifications of this first code of practice to safeguard the rights of a data subject to check that the data is accurate . . .
> . . . we would also be looking for an independent computer expert, trusted by police and the authority, to monitor that the computer is only being used for the purposes in the code.[85]

On this occasion, the authority had, because of its control over the budget, succeeded in influencing the force over an important issue. However, had the chief constable chosen not to co-operate and appealed to the Home Secretary, arguing, perhaps, that by refusing to purchase the new computer the authority was undermining the 'efficiency' of the force, the outcome could have been very different.[86]

The Example of Plastic Bullets and CS Gas

A second illustration of the influence which police authorities can have if they make use of their existing powers came after the announcement in February 1982 that 3,000 plastic bullets (baton rounds) had been distributed to forces in England and Wales. NCCL conducted a survey to find out *which* forces held these weapons, and CS gas, and whether the police authority had made the decision to purchase them; this also revealed wide variations in the approach of the authorities and the extent to which they thought it appropriate to keep the public informed. Finally, questions to the Home Secretary exposed his reluctance to give information to MPs about this controversial development affecting their constituencies.

The questions which the NCCL survey put to the authorities were:

1. Has your force been supplied with plastic bullets and CS gas and, if so, in what quantity?
2. Was the approval of the police authority sought before the supplies were ordered and, if not, was it informed of the decision? Whose decision was it to purchase this equipment?
3. Has the police authority discussed the circumstances in which plastic bullets and CS gas might be used and, if so, what are these circumstances?
4. Are any officers being trained in the use of this equipment and, if so, how many?
5. Have any guidelines on the use of the equipment been issued to these officers and, if so, are these available to the public?

Twenty-three authorities in England and Wales replied, out of forty-three.[87] More than half of these refused to supply all the information, arguing that 'it would be inappropriate for the Police Authority to discuss in public the level and use of police operational practices and equipment' (Avon and Somerset) or simply that 'The use of this equipment is an operational matter and as such is the responsibility of the chief constable' (Sussex). Others were willing to say whether their force held stocks of the equipment but not, for instance, how many officers were trained to use it. While some replies specifically stated that our enquiry had led the authority to raise the matter with the chief constable, Cumbria Authority's chairman went further, replying: '. . . in response to your organisation's attempts to gain information on the matter of CS gas and plastic bullets, I released a press statement locally giving full details of the provision or otherwise of such items to the Cumbria Constabulary'.

Only fourteen replies said or implied that the authority had actually discussed the issue prior to our enquiry. Yet it is now clear from a reply by the Home Secretary to a parliamentary question that some of the authorities which had *not* discussed it did have some or all of the equipment (e.g. Thames Valley (CS gas), Cleveland (CS gas), Sussex (plastic bullets and CS gas)). While Lancashire Police Authority informed us in August 1982 that it had 'not given consideration to this matter', their chief constable reported later in 1982 that public order training had been carried out in that force since the middle of 1981 and the Home Secretary's data shows that Lancashire force does have plastic bullets — though no CS gas.[88]

Some authorities replied that they had specifically approved the equipment (Essex and Lincolnshire), others that they were simply 'consulted' (Suffolk, Avon and Somerset). Devon and Cornwall wrote that such equipment 'would not be purchased without prior consultation with the Police Authority', but Merseyside found that its chief constable had purchased plastic bullets and CS gas, and only informed the authority afterwards.

Merseyside is in fact one of five authorities which have now taken a decision in this regard which has direct implications for operational policing: that the force cannot buy any further stocks of this equipment. Unlike with most operational methods, police authorities may, by refusing to purchase the equipment, prevent their force from using it, thus effectively instructing their chief constable on an operational matter. Nottinghamshire Authority told its chief constable not to purchase any baton rounds, while two authorities which found that this equipment had already been purchased obtained assurances about its use: West Yorkshire accepted an undertaking from the chief constable 'not to use the plastic baton rounds for operational purposes' and requested him 'to arrange for the firing off of existing baton rounds for training purposes only, and to report to the committee when the rounds have been fired off'.[89] Similarly, Derbyshire's chief constable 'gave an undertaking that the twenty baton rounds would be disposed of in training and that further supplies would not be purchased without the Committee's prior approval'. (Significantly, the Home Secretary's data indicates that West Yorkshire and Derbyshire still had plastic bullets in February 1983.) South Yorkshire has since taken a similar decision.

In contrast, those authorities which permitted or approved the purchase of the equipment indicated that the decision to use it was entirely a matter for the chief constable: 'He would only allow the equipment to be used as a last resort and this decision would be taken by the chief constable personally' (Sussex).

It is thus clear from the replies that authorities differ considerably in the extent to which they delegate purchasing powers to their chief constables. Cleveland's chief constable informed his authority in response to our enquiry that his force had held small supplies of CS gas since 1968: 'He could not say where the original authority had come from but supplies had been obtained and replenished from within the normal police budget'. Merseyside's chief constable had clearly felt entitled to purchase the equipment and only inform the authority afterwards.

A Home Office spokesperson, commenting on a suggestion that the Home Office itself had originally supplied the West Yorkshire force with plastic bullets, is reported to have denied this suggestion, saying: 'It's up to the chief officer to decide what equipment he needs'.[90] But the Home Office has explained to the author that the extent of the chief officer's discretion depends on the extent of the authority delegated to him. If there is no budget allocation for riot equipment, he could not purchase any. If he has delegated authority to purchase such equipment (which would cover protective clothing and shields, for instance), an authority hostile to plastic bullets could either advise him not to purchase them but leave the decision to him or withdraw his delegated authority to purchase that kind of equipment. The authority, we were told, holds the purse strings; its authority is 'perfectly real'.

Although it would appear that it is possible for an authority to prevent this equipment being used in its area, such a decision can effectively be overruled for two reasons. First, because its force has a statutory duty to give 'mutual aid' to other forces and, arguably, therefore, has to be in a position to do so. Devon and Cornwall reminded us that the decision is 'relevant to the force's responsibility to assist other forces in emergencies', the implication being that a force lacking such equipment, or not trained to use it, might be considered less capable of providing such mutual aid. The obverse is that a force without plastic bullets could, should rioting occur, receive assistance from a neighbouring force which did have them. Thus, although the West Midlands Authority appears (from the Home Secretary's data) to have decided not to purchase plastic bullets, its force could receive assistance from the neighbouring Warwickshire force which does hold them.

The second, related, reason is that the authority has a duty to maintain an 'adequate and efficient force', and the Home Office (or the courts) could consider that an authority which refused to purchase this equipment was abrogating its responsibility and could supply it directly to the force.

The extent to which the Home Secretary was willing to be open about this issue was demonstrated in his answer to a parliamentary question by David Stoddart MP. When Mr Stoddart asked how many officers in Wiltshire had been trained to use plastic bullets, and whether the Home Secretary would take steps to collect such information for all forces, the reply he received did not even mention Wiltshire:

> Both the extent and the nature of training in the use of this equipment, which is the responsibility of individual chief officers of police, may alter over a brief period. We have no reason to believe that it is necessary to hold centrally details of the numbers of officers trained, in one force or all forces in England and Wales.[91]

'Accountability' in London

Central government's centuries-old desire for greater centralised control over the police has been achieved in its purest form in London, where the 1964 Act did not alter the Home Secretary's role as sole police authority for the Metropolitan Police.

Literally providing no supporting arguments whatsoever, the Royal Commission on the Police had said,

> ... in view of the exceptional police responsibilities in London, control should be in the hands of the Government ... these differences between the control of the police in the Metropolis and elsewhere are broadly justified by the intrinsic importance and interest of events in London which call for police attention.[92]

Consequently, the Home Secretary alone fulfils for the Metropolitan Police the role which a committee of locally elected representatives (and magistrates) plays elsewhere.[93] Neither London borough councillors, nor those elected to the Greater

London Council, have any powers in relation to the Metropolitan Police at all.

A Home Secretary said in 1888 that he was responsible, not for every detail of the management of the Met., but for *the general policy in the discharge of their duty*. The Home Office told the Royal Commission on the Police (RCP) in 1961: 'There has been no change in this general principle'. Yet a recent Home Secretary said that the role he played was only like that of a constitutional monarch, with 'the right to be consulted, the right to warn and the right to encourage':

> I expect the Commissioner to tell me of developments which are likely to be of public interest or which have implications for the force's expenditure, establishment or its relationship with the public. I regard it as part of my function to warn him about anything which is or seems likely to give rise to public criticism ... Equally, I regard it as my duty to encourage the Commissioner in developments which I consider will help the effectiveness of the force and its relations with the public.[94]

Although Home Secretaries have played down their role in this way, both the law and the evidence given to the Royal Commission indicate that their influence is considerably greater than they like to suggest.

The significance of the fact that the relationship between the Home Secretary and the Metropolitan Commissioner is still governed by the 1829 Metropolitan Police Act[95] is that, under section 5 of that Act, the Commissioner must submit any orders and requisitions he makes for the force to the Home Secretary for approval. This, according to the Metropolitan Commissioner in 1961, gives the Home Secretary 'very much wider' powers than his provincial counterparts. These orders, he said, are made 'almost weekly' and the Home Secretary 'frequently' suggests alterations; 'but he does not presume, nor, as I understand the situation, has he the power, to interfere with the Commissioner's discretion in individual or specific decisions on executive matters'. Nevertheless, the Commissioner confirmed that 'practically all matters are referred to the Secretary of State' — a far cry from the relationship between chief constables and their police authorities in the provinces.

Under questioning from the Royal Commission, the Metropolitan Commissioner was unable to explain where the Home Secretary's control stopped and his own began. Asked whether the Home Secretary would consider a new force policy on, say, the enforcement of the Street Offences Act he replied: 'Yes, he would ask us to formulate our views and then he would look at them and if he had any observations to make he would make them and we would come to an agreement on that', adding 'the Assistant Commissioner or another will talk to the Principal of the Home Office about it before it is actually drafted', and concluding: 'I would say he is quite justified in representing to me that my orders directing the way a particular case should be dealt with should be amended, but I would resist any suggestion from him that he would interfere with any particular case'.

When the Commission gave him a particular case as an example, however, that of the 'famous Sidney Street siege', at which the then Home Secretary Winston Churchill had been present, the Metropolitan Commissioner thought the Home Secretary *would* have been able to give orders to the police:

> That is very difficult. I read something the other day saying he [Churchill] never gave a single order, but I think he might on an occasion like that . . . I would have thought that quite fitting for him. If there were much industrial unrest somewhere, that would be a different matter.

Unfortunately, the Commission did not ask him why.[96]

A more recent glimmer of light was thrown on the Home Secretary's role in the debate on 'Policing the Metropolis' in the Commons in February 1983. The Home Secretary reported that he had 'invited' the new Metropolitan Commissioner to prepare a report for him outlining his plans and priorities for the force. He had told him that he 'wished' him to give particular attention to certain areas of concern, including street crime and public order. He had also 'informed' the Commissioner that, as regards the organisation of the force, 'I wished to look to a greater degree of decentralisation to match the development of local consultation on policing'. Sir Kenneth Newman's subsequent report did indeed reflect these requests.[97]

Role of MPs

In exercising his powers as Home Secretary Mr Whitelaw said he paid particular attention to the views put to him by Members of Parliament, especially those from Members representing London constituencies[98] — and it is indeed his accountability to the ninety-two MPs representing London that is often used to justify his position.[99] However, as Chris Price, then MP for Lewisham West, has pointed out, although MPs can probe about with parliamentary questions, 'The trouble is that nobody does it'.[100] He might have added that, when they do, the answers are frequently unsatisfactory.

Successive Home Secretaries have stated that they will only answer questions on operational matters in London which are of 'major public interest', as 'questions relating to the day-to-day operations of the force are for the Commissioner'.[101] Hence, when Harvey Proctor MP asked whether the Home Secretary was satisfied with the provision for the maintenance of law and order in the Brixton area he simply replied: 'The deployment of available resources to particular areas is a matter for the Commissioner of Police of the Metropolis'.[102]

A recent survey of parliamentary questions on the Metropolitan Police over a two-month period revealed that the then Home Secretary had refused to answer one sixth of all the questions because of 'cost' or because the information was 'not in the public interest'. The author of the survey rightly concluded that there were limitations to the practice of calling the Home Secretary to account through the mechanism of parliamentary questions. It also led him to ask: on what grounds does the Home Office have the right to decide that the cost of providing the information would be too great, or that it would be 'not in the public interest'?[103]

Like provincial police authorities, the Home Secretary can demand a report from the Metropolitan Commissioner, or set up an enquiry, but he rarely responds to MPs' requests for him to do so.[104] When he does call for a report, as into the police raid in Railton Road, Brixton, on 15 July 1981, MPs may feel his subsequent report to Parliament is quite inadequate, but they cannot insist that more information is provided or that the Commissioner change his policies or practices in future. The reports are not usually published.[105]

The net result of the ambiguity and secrecy surrounding the role and responsibilities of the Home Secretary in relation to the Metropolitan Police is that even London MPs are left unsure who actually makes the crucial decisions. Alf Dubs, MP for Battersea South, has explained:

> Let's take obstruction. There are quite a number of incidences [*sic*] recorded where a traditional left wing newspaper seller, who goes to the same place week after week, suddenly gets picked up for obstruction . . . There are incidences where people get picked up for standing next to a newspaper seller of the ordinary kind, the ordinary newspaper seller not being touched by the police . . . In London one can only complain to the Home Secretary. This I have done on one occasion, but the Home

Secretary said that it was a matter for local discretion and why didn't I get my constituent to make an official complaint? ...

... [I think] it is quite probable that the Home Office had nothing to do with it, that there's been no Home Office directive or anything like that. It is equally possible that the chief constables, the police officers themselves, have got together and quite informally have said, 'Look, there are too many of these Revolutionary Communist Party newspaper sellers, let's have a go and just not have them all standing about there, let's just shift them, move them along a bit'.

I'm only speculating, I have no evidence at all. *The thing is, I can't discover whether that's the way it works or not, because they operate in secret where they can make their decisions and they're not accountable*. That itself is a threat to democracy because you have people with a lot of power who can exercise it in a way which is not responsive to any elected politician, which is not even responsive to the Home Office. That, to me, is dangerous.[106] [our emphasis].

Mr Dubs noted, in the debate on the Metropolitan Police in February 1983, that it was a historic occasion — the first time the House had ever had the chance to devote a full day to a debate on that subject. Roy Hattersley, speaking for the Labour opposition, welcomed the debate as 'the nearest we ever get under the present law to influencing the policy of the Metropolitan Police'.[107]

Inspections

The Metropolitan Police has never been inspected, as the provincial forces are, by HM Inspectorate of Constabulary. Since 1979, inspections have been carried out internally by a department headed by a deputy assistant commissioner, sections of the force being checked in a three-year cycle. The reports are sent to the Home Secretary. When the first cycle was completed in 1981, sixty-nine reports were sent, covering twenty-four districts. The 'keynotes' of the inspections are reported to be cost-effectiveness and police-public relations.[108]

Finance

Like provincial forces, half the Metropolitan Police's income comes from local and half from central government. London boroughs, however, and the surrounding councils which fall within the Metropolitan Police boundaries, must raise the sum demanded by the Metropolitan Police Receiver while having no say over the total amount or how it is spent. Since 1949 the receiver, who is appointed by the Crown, has agreed to meet two representatives of the Borough Treasurers informally to discuss his demand, but they cannot veto the sum the Home Secretary has approved. Consequently, there is no public debate about the budget nor any public explanation of the proposed expenditure. No time is allocated for a parliamentary debate on the issue and the Commissioner's annual report provides little detail on the force's expenditure.

London ratepayers had to find £198 million for the year 1983-4, a precept of 11.06p in the pound. Statistics published by CIPFA[109] show that the Metropolitan Police is the most expensive force in the country, costing almost double the average for other large cities.[110]

On all counts, from its low crime clear-up rate to its status as the force which receives the most complaints, the Metropolitan Police is often considered poor value for money.[111] But London ratepayers are also obliged to pay for national policing duties, such as policing demonstrations and guarding embassies, because these occur in the capital. Since 1909, central government has contributed an 'Imperial and National Services Grant' to cover these services. But the grant, which for 1983-4 was £13.1 million, falls far short of the £24 million which the Home Office itself estimated it cost to maintain these services in 1981-2[112].

The exclusion of local councillors

London's councillors have no statutory powers or responsibilities in relation to the Metropolitan Police, and it was not until the dramatic evidence of the breakdown in the relationship between the police and sections of the public in 1981 that the Home Secretary actively encouraged their participation in consultative arrangements. The editor of *Police* wrote in 1976:

> It is an odd feature of our police arrangements that the Metropolitan Police operate without any vestige of local control . . . Here is a classic example of taxation without representation, yet the prospects of changing the position are remote. *There is surprising unanimity between both main parties in London local government that some form of democratically elected police authority for the Metropolitan Police is desirable.* The reaction of Conservative and Labour Home Secretaries to such an idea has been the same, hostile and contemptuous [our emphasis].[113]

London councillors' criticism of their lack of powers over the

Metropolitan Police has historically focused on their lack of control over the budget, taking up the cry of 'no taxation without representation'. What the London Liberal Radical Union argued in 1882 remains true today:

> The London police force are the dearest police in England. The people of London have no control over them at all. They are managed by the Home Office which is not responsible to the London ratepayers. Every other great town has the control of its own police . . . London has the same right and the same need for the control of its own police as any other great town.[114]

Borough councillors' frustration at their inability to influence the policing of their borough led Lewisham Council to threaten, in 1980, to refuse to pay its share of the bill the following year until senior officers 'demonstrate a more appropriate application of their resources to, and awareness of, the needs of the people of London generally and Lewisham in particular'. Moreover, it demanded that 'the Commissioner and his subordinates cease to exploit the irresponsible position in which the current legislation places them and urge the Home Secretary to end the immunity that the Metropolitan Police enjoy from the scrutiny of the ratepayers and their elected representatives'.[115]

The council's action was prompted by dissatisfaction with police priorities, including a recent decision to close a police station in Sydenham, their low crime clear-up rate, and the local commander's refusal to ask the Home Secretary to ban National Front marches through the area. According to Councillor Dowd, who moved the motion:

> We want to know that the money is being spent in the most productive way. The police in London are run solely by policemen . . . it is a unique situation that we would not tolerate in any other field. In health and education there is an amalgam of people behind the professionals. So it should be with the police . . . Catford has the worst burglary figures in the country. Lewisham is snarled up with traffic problems. Our car and house insurance rates are the highest in London. The police turn around and say they haven't the manpower . . . yet they spend half a million pounds allowing 200 nazis and 800 juvenile thugs to march in our streets.[116]

Lewisham was not alone in complaining loudly at this time. Councillors in Wandsworth, Southwark and Lambeth were also considering withholding their precept, while some of the councils outside the GLC area but wholly or partly within the Metropolitan Police area were considering the feasibility of pulling out. Epsom and Ewell had set up a working party to consider this move, one argument being that the high cost of policing demonstrations in central London meant that the fringe boroughs did not get value for money. The chair of the council's finance committee told *The Times*:

> . . . there is considerable dissatisfaction with the level of control over policing in our areas, probably similar to that in Lewisham. The difference is that Lewisham do not have the same choice. Their decision was to withhold payment. Ours would be to move into Surrey.[117]

Had Lewisham refused to pay the £5.5 million demanded by the Metropolitan Police Receiver the following April, each councillor could have been liable to a surcharge of £147,000, and this may have influenced their eventual decision to pay up.[118] Significantly, the Commander of Lewisham District was moved out of the borough in May and replaced by a man said to be more willing to listen to the public's views, a not infrequent response to stem public criticism of a particular officer. A Lewisham councillor told *Rights* in September 1981 that the council had been divided over whether they should pay up but had been swayed by the failure of other London boroughs to follow their lead, and by the expectation of the election of a Labour-held GLC which 'would continue the fight in a more co-ordinated way with other local councils joining in'.[119]

Hackney Council has also wielded the threat of refusing to pay the precept, to back up its demand that the Home Secretary establish an enquiry into the death of Colin Roach.

Colin Roach, a 21-year-old black man, died on 12 January 1983 in the foyer of Stoke Newington police station from a shotgun blast. The police later announced that he had committed suicide; his family and many of the black community said publicly that they believed he was murdered.[120]

Local MP Ernie Roberts sought Parliament's backing for an enquiry, expressing grave concern, in an Early Day Motion, 'about the breakdown of relations between the police and public in the Hackney-Stoke Newington area, which has been brought to crisis point by the death of Colin Roach in Stoke Newington Police Station and the subsequent arrest of 70 persons [at demonstrations] . . . and urging the Home Secretary to make an investigation into the policing practices in Hackney-Stoke Newington'.

Hackney Council passed an emergency motion calling on the

Home Secretary to set up an enquiry, and emphasised its demand by agreeing, on 23 February, 'That the Council take whatever steps are open to it to withhold the payment of the police precept both as an expression of anger at the state of policing in Hackney and with a view to bringing home to the Government the community demands for an independent enquiry into policing in Hackney'.[121] The police precept of approximately £4 million was due on 7 April, and the council's officers were instructed to investigate the options open to the council for withholding it.

The council was advised that its refusal to pay the precept would amount to neglect of statutory duty and, after a six-week period of grace, would make it liable to pay interest on the sum withheld at 2 per cent above base rate. The police could ask the minister for a certificate stating that 'the rating authority have refused, either through wilful neglect or wilful default, to pay the amount due under the precept', which would then enable the police to appoint a receiver to obtain the money from the council by deducting it from the central government block grant to the borough. The police could also ask the court for an order of *mandamus* to make the council pay the precept, an action it could take before or after the money was withheld. Moreover, councillors would personally be liable to surcharge to cover the police's legal costs.[122]

Aware that it had no legal right to withhold the precept, the council had carefully worded the resolution to avoid stating that it would actually do so, the intention being to use the threat to emphasise the extent of their concern. Councillor Heaven said: 'We have done everything we possibly could within the constraints of the law. The police precept won't be paid until they are actually threatening to close down the council. It will very clearly be seen to be paid under duress'.[123]

The Home Secretary did not consent to set up the enquiry. While agreeing that a full examination of the cause of Colin Roach's death was needed, it insisted that the inquest would 'provide the forum for such an investigation'.

While Hackney Council was in dispute with the Home Secretary over his refusal to set up an enquiry, it was also negotiating on another issue: the form, if any, which a police-community consultative committee should take in the borough.

Lord Scarman's report on the Brixton disturbances, in which he commented that the Metropolitan Police 'are nationally, but not locally, accountable',[124] had prompted the Home Office to rethink the role local councillors should play. Lord Scarman noted that in London no committee drawn from the community had the right to receive a report from the police or to lay down any requirements, and that this enabled the police to ignore local opinion.

Nevertheless, Scarman reasserted the Royal Commission's view, again without any supporting arguments, that the Home Secretary should remain the sole police authority for London, and insisted only that there needed to be 'more effective channels of communication' between the police and the people — that is, consultative or 'liaison' committees at borough level.

Scarman had the lesson of one such liaison committee before him when he wrote his report. A first meeting of a committee bringing together the Council for Community Relations in Lambeth (CCRL) and the commander of the local police district had taken place on 30 October 1978. The minutes were to be confidential, and the commander had made it clear that responsibility for policing the area was his and that he would use whatever resources were available to him.

Three days later, the commander launched a special operation against street crime using the special patrol group (SPG) and local officers. He had not informed the liaison committee because he feared that 'news of it might become public and its effectiveness would be diminished', an omission which 'greatly angered some of the community leaders'.[125] The object of the operation was to saturate the area with police officers who would frequently stop people and search them. The long-term beneficial effect on crime was, Scarman says, very questionable, and the effect on police-community relations beyond doubt: it provoked the hostility of young black people, 'who felt they were being hunted irrespective of their innocence or guilt'. Their hostility, he wrote, infected older members of the community, who themselves began to lose confidence in, and respect for, the police. However well-intentioned, Scarman concluded, these operations precipitated a crisis of confidence between the police and certain community leaders. In particular they led to a breakdown of the formal arrangements for liaison between the ethnic minority communities, the local authority, and the police.[126]

At the second meeting of the committee, in January 1979, the operation was not even discussed. Before the third meeting, the 'sheepskin coat' incident, in which three members of the CCRL staff were arrested and questioned about an assault in a Clapham pub, prompted the CCRL to withdraw from the committee altogether. The police attempted to re-start the meetings, but the CCRL refused, saying: 'Our experience of liaison with the police has been that it is totally ineffective in establishing constructive dialogue'.[127] A subsequent report by a working party set up by Lambeth Council to examine community-police relations in Lambeth concluded: 'The evidence is that the terms of reference of liaison committees are without any real power'.[128]

Scarman's conclusion was, however, very different. He concluded that the problem was that the liaison committees were only on a voluntary basis: 'the difficulty about voluntary arrangements', he wrote, was that 'they depend too much on the willingness of all parties to participate; if, for any reason, a local difficulty prompts one of the parties to withdraw, the arrangement collapses and discussion stops'.[129] He therefore recommended that 'a statutory framework be developed to *require* local consultation between the Metropolitan Police and the Community', a proposal which later prompted the government to impose on the Metropolitan Commissioner a duty to make arrangements to consult the public, in its Police and Criminal Evidence Act. In the interim, the Home Secretary issued, in June 1982, guidelines to the Metropolitan Commissioner (and police authorities outside London) urging them to set up voluntary local consultative arrangements.[130]

Consultation with the public had earned just one paragraph in the Metropolitan Commissioner's annual report for 1981. At the end of the year which had seen the worst clashes between the police and sections of the community for many years, the Commissioner reported: 'In general liaison with the boroughs themselves, both centrally and locally, which I have fostered over the years, has never been better. In some 17 boroughs formal liaison committees exist; in most others the communications between local senior officers and the elected and permanent local authority officials are very good'.[131]

The Commissioner's concern to foster such liaison does not appear to have been shared by at least one of his senior officers, then Commander of G District. In response to repeated criticism from the leader of Hackney Council that his use of the SPG in the area was unnecessary and provocative, Commander Mitchell said on TV: 'I don't feel obliged to tell anyone about my policing activities . . . we have to be totally cut off from the politics of it'.[132]

The London Borough Council elections in May 1982 had resulted in the election of a number of Labour councils committed, like the Greater London Council elected the previous year, to campaigning for democratic control over London's police and to establishing, for the first time, their own police committee, as an interim measure until a statutory police authority comprised of locally elected representatives was established.[133]

By the end of the year a number of boroughs, including Hackney, Camden, Islington, Southwark, Greenwich and Haringey, had established committees (see chapter 6). One of the first questions Hackney Police Committee had to resolve was its response to the Home Secretary's request that they establish consultative arrangements with their local force. The guidelines stressed that any liaison committee that was established would be for consultation only and would not affect the independence of the police. The police would be in no way accountable to that committee.

Under the previous Labour administration, members of the council's top committee, Policy and Resources, had met periodically with the commander of the local police force, in private. The police hoped that this arrangement would continue and that the council would consider favourably the proposals for new consultative machinery from the Home Office.[134]

The new police committee concluded at its first meeting, however, that this liaison group 'had failed to make headway on major issues such as use of the special patrol group and the "Sus" laws and other sensitive issues'. Instead, the committee proposed to set up a subcommittee on which the police would be invited to participate, but with no voting rights. The subcommittee would (normally) be open to the public and press. The terms of reference of the subcommittee were to be 'to investigate and report upon specific matters at the request of the police committee and to provide a means of liaison and consultation with the Metropolitan Police'.[135]

The council subsequently wrote to Commander Howlett in July inviting the police to participate on these terms. Commander Howlett referred the request to the Home Office, which informed the council in September that 'The council's present proposals do create certain difficulties for the police where they depart substantially from the guidelines approved by the Home Secretary'.[136]

After a series of meetings and correspondence, Home Office Minister David Waddington finally rejected the council's proposals in March 1983. Mr Waddington's objection was:

> We continue to see difficulty in the group taking the form of a subcommittee of the Borough Council, since this must imply that its membership collectively is answerable to the local authority. You will appreciate that, under the present arrangements for policing London, the Metropolitan Police cannot be put in that position. Nor would it be acceptable for Members of Parliament or GLC councillors. No consultative arrangements should be so dominated in form or representation by any one body that it fails to reflect the quality of membership acceptable for sensible consultation.[137]

Other London boroughs have adopted a very different approach, some councils welcoming the consultative arrangements, if not always with the wide community representation recommended by the Home Secretary.[138]

Conclusion

How accountable are the police to our elected representatives? The 1964 Police Act placed each force under the *control* of its chief constable. But it did not, in turn, place chief constables under the control of elected representatives. Nor did it make chief constables genuinely *accountable* to elected representatives if, by accountable, we mean that the elected representatives can discipline a chief constable if they disapprove of his actions. The powers of elected representatives are very limited in this respect. The Act did make chief constables accountable to the law, but the courts have chosen only to intervene in extreme circumstances if the police totally fail to enforce the law: they will not tell them *how* to enforce it.

The powers of police authorities, the Home Secretary, and chief constables overlap, and their respective jurisdictions are unclear. Although policing policy decisions are crucial to the 'efficiency' of the force (and may be political and have major implications for the ratepayers), they come under the control of the chief constable. Although it is the police authorities, and not the Home Secretary, which are responsible for maintaining 'an adequate and efficient force', the Home Secretary's influence over policing developments is far greater.

Police authorities have few powers and almost all of their actions are subject to the approval of the Home Secretary. In practice, many appear to have chosen not to exercise fully the powers they do have, being content to rubber-stamp the decisions of their chief constables. Those few authorities which have attempted to influence their chief constable have had limited success. If he chose to do so, the Home Secretary could overrule their decisions in favour of the chief constable. Confidence that the 'tripartite' system genuinely divides control evenly between the authorities, chief constables and the Home Secretary is therefore misplaced.

The chief constable is not in practice accountable to the police authority; neither is the authority genuinely accountable to its electorate. First, one third of the authority, the magistrates, are not elected but appointed, and are not even expected to be accountable. Yet if they vote with a minority opposition on the authority, they can undermine democracy by outvoting the majority.

Secondly, the available evidence shows that many authorities have seen their role as representing the police to the public, rather than the public's interests to the police. Because representing the interests of the public in relation to policing has not been seen as part of their role, the local political parties have not usually included their proposals for policing in their election manifesto, and not all police authority meetings have been open to the public. The public cannot, therefore, in any sense call their authority to account.

The extent of the Home Secretary's influence over policing developments relative to that of chief constables is impossible to quantify, in part because of the obsessive secrecy which surrounds his consultations with them, in part because his decisions and those of his department are not subject to close parliamentary scrutiny. Where a chief constable breaks Home Office guidelines (as in the use of CS gas in Merseyside) or provides inaccurate information in a report, the Home Secretary does not necessarily call him to account. Like police authorities, successive Home Secretaries appear to have seen their role primarily as supporting chief constables rather than representing the interests of the public.

No other body can call the police to account. County councils have very limited powers over the police authorities; chief constables are not subject to investigation by the Ombudsman (although police authorities are), and the Director of Public Prosecution's influence is limited to authorising prosecution for a number of offences and issuing guidelines.

This lack of accountability is most acute in London, where there is no locally elected police authority, only the Home Secretary. Although London MPs are sometimes more successful than their provincial colleagues in obtaining information about the policing of their area, the Home Secretary does not report regularly to Parliament in the way that police authorities are expected to do to their county council; and London councillors have no powers whatsoever. For London ratepayers there is, literally, taxation without representation. Yet the Home Secretary's relationship with the Metropolitan Commissioner, were the veil of secrecy to be removed, would be seen to be far closer, and the Home Secretary's influence far greater, than that of police authorities outside London.

Under the 1964 Act, chief constables were never intended to be genuinely accountable for their actions. But both police authorities and Home Secretaries have neglected to use the powers they were given to call their chief constables to account. To say that chief constables are not accountable for their actions is not, therefore, to hold them solely responsible for that situation. Many police authorities and successive Home Secretaries have, by failing to fulfil their responsibilities, participated in a situation grounded in the 1964 Act and used by chief constables confident of their ability to make the right decisions. Not only have the elected representatives often failed to call the police to account; they themselves have not been genuinely accountable to the public for their actions. Remedies for this dual lack of accountability will be considered in chapter 5. In the next chapter, however, we will examine the arguments put forward by those who wish to maintain the status quo.

Notes

1. *New Society*, 18 February 1982.
2. *The Guardian*, 21 September 1981.
3. *New Society*, 17 July 1980.
4. *Ibid*.
5. Interviewed on 'The Police and the Public', *Weekend World*, 23 March 1980.
6. 'A Police Authority — the Denial of Conflict', *Sociological Review*, Vol.25, No.2 (May 1977), p.331.
7. *Ibid*. p.330.
8. *Worcester Evening News*, 12 December 1979.
9. For an analysis of the issues relating to police authorities raised by the miners' dispute see Sarah Spencer, 'The Eclipse of the Police Authority', in Bob Fine and Robert Millar (ed), *Policing the Miners' Strike*, Lawrence and Wishart, 1985.
10. *Hansard*, 15 April 1981, col.142. Unfortunately *Hansard* records no details of the incident.
11. Richard Card, 'Police Accountability and Control over the Police', *Bramshill Journal*, Vol.1, No.1 (Autumn 1979).
12. *Hansard*, 26 November 1963, col.205.
13. *Ibid*., col.86.
14. *Ibid*., col.87.
15. Merlyn Rees, *Hansard*, June 1978.
16. *Rights* (Spring 1983).
17. Peter Taylor, *Beating the Terrorists* (Penguin, 1980).
18. Dr A.L. Goodhart, *Report of the Royal Commission on the Police*, (HMSO, May 1962), Cmnd 1728, para.58.
19. See below, p.65.
20. 'Survey of Matters of Practice on Police Authorities' conducted by the Working Party of the ACC and AMA (1976). Published in *Role and Responsibilities of the Police Authority* (Merseyside Police Authority, 1980).
21. *New Society*, 17 July 1980.
22. Correspondence between the author and NCCL Northumberland and Durham group, August-October 1980; letter from Councillor R. Hall, Chairman of the Authority, to Jean Rogers, Secretary of the Northumberland and Durham NCCL group, 5 September 1980; letter from Assistant Chief Constable, Cleveland Constabulary, to Jean Rogers, dated 17 October 1980; minutes of the meeting of the police authority as presented to Cleveland County Council on 22 October 1980.
23. See p.59.
24. This account of the procedure was given by a member of the authority to two members of NCCL's Northumberland and Durham group.

25. Account given by a member of the authority interviewed by the author, June 1984.
26. *Hansard*, 26 November 1963, col.205.
27. *State Research Bulletin*, No.29 (April/May 1982), and internal NCCL correspondence.
28. Letter from Councillor Luff to Somerset NCCL group dated 21 May 1982 and internal NCCL correspondence.
29. Notes on seminar held in London on 16 and 17 March 1977, published in *Role and Responsibilities of the Police Authority*, *op.cit.*
30. *New Society*, 17 July 1980.
31. Brogden 1977 *op.cit.*, p.332.
32. Interviewed on 'The Police and the Public', *Weekend World*, 23 March 1980.
33. *The Times*, 13 April 1982.
34. *The Times*, 1 April 1982.
35. *Middlesborough Evening Gazette*, 6 July 1982.
36. Interview with Councillor Taylor, chairman of Nottinghamshire Authority, October 1984.
37. 'Survey of Matters of Practice on Police Authorities', *op.cit.*
38. Letter from Margaret Simey to NCCL, 9 October 1979.
39. Conversation with the author, June 1984.
40. Richard Card, *op.cit.*
41. *Hansard*, 13 July 1979.
42. *Hansard*, 11 May 1981, col.170.
43. *Hansard*, 5 March 1981, col.155.
44. *Hansard*, 2 March 1981, col.142.
45. *Hansard*, 19 October 1981.
46. *New Statesman*, 25 June 1982.
47. *The Observer*, 21 January 1983.
48. Report of Inquiry by Mr A.E. James QC into the circumstances in which it was possible for Detective Sergeant Harold Gordon Challenor of the Metropolitan Police to continue on duty at a time when he appears to have been affected by the onset of mental illness. Cmnd 2735 (HMSO 1965).
49. The Red Lion Square Disorders of the 15th of June 1974. Report of an Inquiry by Lord Justice Scarman. Cmnd 5919 (HMSO 1975).
50. *The Brixton Disorders 10-12 April 1981*. Report of an Inquiry by the Rt. Hon. The Lord Scarman OBE. Cmnd 8427 (HMSO 1981).
51. Report of an Inquiry by the Hon. Sir Henry Fisher into the circumstances leading to the trial of three persons on charges arising out of the death of Maxwell Confait and the fire at 27 Doggett Road, London SE6 (HMSO, 1977).
52. *Hansard*, 26 November 1963, col.96.
53. *Report of Her Majesty's Chief Inspector of Constabulary* (HMSO, 1981). See the *Sunday Times* of 25 March 1984 on the role of this unit in the 1984 miners' industrial dispute.
54. *The Times*, 2 June 1981.
55. *Report of the Royal Commission on the Police*, *op.cit.*, Appendix 11 to the Minutes of Evidence, p.8.
56. *Ibid.*, pp.31-2.
57. See chapter 4.
58. *State Research Bulletin* No.19 (August/September 1980), p.148.
59. Martin Kettle in Peter Hain (ed.), *Policing the Police*, Vol.2 (John Calder, 1980), p.45. See also the article by the same author in the *Sunday Times*, 25 March 1984, on the role of the president of ACPO as national co-ordinator of the mutual aid arrangements at Scotland Yard during the 1984 miners' dispute: 'The important role played by Hall has highlighted the emergence of ACPO as a key body in the gradual centralisation of parts of Britain's policing system'.

60. *Report of Her Majesty's Chief Inspector of Constabulary* (HMSO, 1979), Cmnd 725, para.6.3.
61. *New Society*, 17 July 1980.
62. Duncan Campbell in Peter Hain, *op.cit.*, p.85.
63. *Ibid.*, p.93.
64. *Hansard*, 2 December 1977.
65. Duncan Campbell in Peter Hain, *op.cit.*, p.77.
66. *Ibid.*, p.80.
67. *Ibid.*, p.140.
68. *Report of Her Majesty's Chief Inspector of Constabulary* (HMSO, 1978), Cmnd 1351, p.42.
69. *Hansard*, 6 April 1978.
70. Patricia Hewitt, *The Abuse of Power* (Martin Robertson, 1981), p.31. It is clear that the Special Branch do indeed maintain surveillance of people who are involved in lawful political activities, viz. the case of Madelaine Haigh who was visited by the Special Branch after she wrote to her local paper arguing against the siting of cruise missiles in Britain. *The Guardian*, 20 September 1983.
71. *Rights*, Vol.3, No.4.
72. *Newsline*, 3 October 1979.
73. Letter from Margaret Simey to NCCL, 12 September 1979.
74. *The Economist*, 13 October 1979.
75. *Liverpool Daily Post*, 19 October 1979.
76. Quoted in the *Liverpool Echo*, 19 May 1980.
77. *The Times*, 7 January 1980.
78. *The Guardian*, 21 November 1979; *The Times*, 7 January 1980.
79. *The Guardian*, 14 January 1980.
80. Phil Scraton and Paul Gordon, *Causes for Concern* (Penguin, 1984), from which some of this account of events in Merseyside is drawn.
81. Merseyside County Labour Party Manifesto (County Council Elections, 1981).
82. Home Secretary Frank Soskice, statement to the House of Commons in 1965 (our emphasis).
83. *Sunday Telegraph*, 13 September 1981.
84. Margaret Simey addressing a conference on policing at the Polytechnic of Central London, 4 October 1981.
85. *Daily Telegraph*, 19 September 1981. In the event the authority decided in September 1984 to block the purchase of the criminal records computer system for three reasons: cost, the failure of the police to agree to local monitoring, and duplication of functions with the Police National Computer. *Computing The Newspaper*, 4 October 1984.
86. See also *State Research Bulletin* No.31 (August/September 1982); *The Guardian*, 1 December 1983.
87. Interim results were published in *Rights*, Vol.6, No.6 (October/December 1982).
88. *Hansard*, 1 February 1983, col.61-2, and *Hansard*, 5 December 1983.
89. Minutes of meeting of the West Yorkshire Police Authority, 30 July 1982.
90. *New Statesman*, 23 July 1982.
91. *Hansard*, 25 February 1983, col.549.
92. *Report of the Royal Commission on the Police*, *op.cit.*, paras.223 and 225.
93. The Metropolitan Commissioner is officially appointed by the Queen, however. See *Hansard*, 27 July 1982, col.444.
94. William Whitelaw's address to the joint ACPO-Local Authority Association Conference. Eastbourne, 10 June 1981.
95. As amended by the 1968 Justices of the Peace Act and 1973 Administration of Justice Act.
96. Minutes of Evidence to the Royal Commission on the Police, *op.cit.*, vol.20:

The Metropolitan Commissioner.
97. *Hansard*, 28 February 1983, cols.23 and 29.
98. William Whitelaw's address of 10 June 1981, *op.cit.*
99. See, for example, GLC Councillor Lemkin, Conservative spokesman on the police, *Daily Telegraph*, 5 August 1981.
100. *The Leveller*, 17 April 1981. A survey of parliamentary questions on the Metropolitan Police showed that in a two-month period the Home Secretary was asked 58 questions by 32 MPs. Only 18 of London's 92 MPs were amongst them. See note 12.
101. *Hansard*, 8 February 1983, col.312.
102. *Hansard*, 28 July 1982, col.531.
103. Survey by Steve Bassam, *Policing London* 7 (April/May 1983); *The Guardian*, 25 April 1983. The survey covered the period from 6 December 1982 to 4 February 1983. See also the *New Statesman*, 6 May 1983.
104. E.g. demands from Liberal MPs for an enquiry into corruption, *Hansard*, 18 November 1982, col.403.
105. See, e.g., *Hansard*, 27 January 1983, col.490.
106. Interview published in *Poly Law Review*, Vol.6, No.2 (Spring 1981), pp.4 and 15.
107. *Hansard*, 28 February 1983, cols.93 and 31.
108. *The Times*, 3 January 1983.
109. Chartered Institute of Public Finance and Accountancy.
110. Chartered Institute of Public Finance and Accountancy. Quoted by Steve Bundred in Cowell *et al.* (ed.), *Policing the Riots* (Junction Books, 1982), p.59.
111. *Ibid.*, pp.58-64.
112. *Hansard*, 27 January 1983, col.489, and 21 February 1983, col.307.
113. *Police*, Vol.IX, No.1 (September/October 1976).
114. Quoted in Bundred, *op.cit.*, p.59.
115. Minutes of the meeting of Lewisham Borough Council, 16 April 1980.
116. *Evening Standard*, 17 April 1980; *South London Press*, 15 April 1980.
117. *The Times*, 19 April 1980.
118. *The Leveller*, 17 April 1981.
119. *Rights*, Vol.6, No.1 (September/October 1981), Councillor Russell Proffitt.
120. See *Hackney Gazette*, 14 January 1983, and later issues (twice weekly) between January and March.
121. Minutes of the meeting of Hackney Borough Council held on 23 February 1983.
122. 1967 General Rate Act s.2(1), s.11, s.12(2), s.12(3), s.12(8), s.12(9), s.15; The Precepts (Rate of Interest) Rules 1982 (pursuant to s.42(3) of the Local Government Act 1974); s.161 Local Government Act 1972; *Asher* v. *Lacey* (1973) 1 WLR 1412.
123. *Hackney Gazette*, 11 March 1983.
124. Lord Scarman, *The Brixton Disorders 10-12 April 1981,* Cmnd 8427, para.5.67.
125. *Ibid.*, para.4.25.
126. *Ibid.*, para.4.22.
127. *Ibid.*, para.4.36.
128. *Final Report of the Working Party on Community-Police Relations in Lambeth* (London Borough of Lambeth, January 1981).
129. Scarman Report, *op.cit.*, para.5.69.
130. See chapter 4 for details of these guidelines.
131. *Report of the Commissioner of Police of the Metropolis for the year 1981*, Cmnd 8569, p.6.
132. *In Evidence: The Sharp End*, ITV, 25 June 1980.
133. See, for example, Hackney Labour Party Manifesto, May 1982.

134. Letter from Commander Howlett to council leader Anthony Kendall, 1 June 1982.
135. Report of the police committee meeting held on 8 July 1982.
136. Letter from the Home Office to Hackney's chief executive, 28 September 1982.
137. Letter from David Waddington to Councillor Kendall, 4 March 1983.
138. *Policing London* 7 (April/May 1983).

CHAPTER 4
In Defence of the Status Quo

Senior police officers and the present government have been united in resisting the now widespread calls for greater accountability. They believe, in the words of the Chief Constable of Greater Manchester, that 'The police service, immune from the ideological pressure of any single political party, provides the surest and only guarantee of the people's individual freedom'. Unless the present independence and impartiality of the police can be preserved, he wrote, then the struggle for our traditional democracy will be over: 'If some of the new proposals affecting police accountability were introduced the character of the British police would be changed for ever and life in this country would never be the same again'.[1]

There are five arguments which are used to defend the existing relationship between the police, the law and elected representatives:

1. The police have a duty to enforce the law impartially and it would therefore be dangerous for them to be subject to the direction of individuals who may have vested interests or hold particular views. In the words of *Police*, the journal of the Police Federation: 'Those who campaign for stronger powers for police authorities are, whether they appreciate it or not, attacking the principle of a strictly impartial and independent police service'.[2]
2. The police are already accountable to the law.
3. The police are professionals with special expertise and an ability to exercise sound professional judgement.
4. The police are accountable to elected representatives.
5. The police are accountable to the public itself.

We will consider each of these arguments in turn.

1. Impartial Law Enforcement

On joining the police force each new constable takes an oath to carry out his duties 'without favour or affection, malice or ill-will'. Constables are not allowed to take an active part in politics[3] nor to become MPs,[4] and the Police Discipline Code places further restrictions on constables taking part, when off duty, in activities which the public might feel conflict with their impartiality. The police are particularly concerned to be seen to be impartial in enforcing the law, Sir Kenneth Newman arguing in a recent paper, for example, that, the observance of 'due process' (e.g. observing correct procedures to protect suspects' civil liberties) is central to the appearance of police impartiality and should therefore be given prominence in policy statements.[5]

This declaration of impartiality is, however, in direct conflict with the police's own recognition, and society's acceptance, that the police do not interpret their duty to enforce the law in the same way on each occasion. As Lord Scarman concluded from his enquiry into the Brixton disorders:

> ... the exercise of discretion lies at the heart of the policing function. It is undeniable that there is only one law for all: and it is right that this should be so. But it is equally well recognised that successful policing depends on the exercise of discretion in how the law is enforced. The good reputation of the police as a force depends upon the skill and judgement which policemen display in the particular circumstances of the cases and incidents which they are required to handle. Discretion is the art of suiting action to particular circumstances. It is the policeman's daily task.[6]

Scarman emphasised that it is right for the police to use their discretion to enforce the law selectively to support his recommendation that the police's highest priority should be maintaining order rather than enforcing the law, a view which Sir Kenneth Newman has endorsed, arguing: '. . . it is a contradiction when the law is enforced in a way which promotes disorder and furthers lawlessness. The need is for discretion, sensitive judgement and professional skill in enforcing the law accurately and selectively'.[7]

Scarman and Newman were referring both to the discretion exercised by constables on the street and to that exercised by the senior officers in charge of the operation who issue the instructions. The response by chief constables to the introduction of the new seat-belt law on 31 January 1983 provides a striking illustration of the extent of *their* discretion in determining law enforcement priorities for their force. A survey of forces throughout Britain revealed that while some intended to prosecute seat-belt offenders immediately, others intended only to warn offenders and give advice about the law. While Merseyside's chief constable's view was that 'we just have not got the resources to prosecute everyone and I believe it would be self-destructive' the chief constable of Kent force believed that 'to ignore it . . . would be to condone the death and injury which occurs daily on our roads. This is something no police officer can tolerate on his conscience'.[8] Surrey and West Yorkshire forces announced that they would stop offenders, advise them of the law, and give them a 'belt-up' sticker for their dashboard, and Strathclyde similarly said that they 'intended to educate rather than to prosecute'. In contrast, Gloucestershire said, 'There will be no honeymoon period here'.[9]

The fact that chief constables have this degree of discretion means that the impact of any piece of legislation is largely determined by the police rather than by Parliament, police authorities or the courts.

A further, and more controversial, example of the extent of police discretion is provided by the use of the 'Sus' law to prosecute those 'loitering with intent to commit an arrestable offence'. Statistics showing how many people in each force area were taken to court on a 'Sus' charge illustrate a vast difference in the use of this law even between forces facing similar crime problems. Thus while Merseyside came top of the poll, with the Metropolitan Police a close second, the latter used the 'Sus' charges three times more often than the police in Greater Manchester. Similarly, in London 'Sus' was used more often in some boroughs than in others.[10] The fact that the police used their discretion to arrest disproportionately more black people for 'Sus' offences than white people was a major factor leading to opposition to the law and its eventual repeal in 1981.

Criticism of the police has often focused on their use of their discretion — the way in which they have handled demonstrations, civil disturbances, domestic disputes or racist attacks to take a few examples. In practice, police use of their discretion has not always resulted in fair, unprejudiced or impartial policing.

This criticism does not imply that the public expects the police to give equal priority to every law and treat each suspect in the same way. If only because of the shortage of resources, they have to enforce the law selectively; and it is also desirable that they should do so. The enforcement of some laws *is* more important than others. The question is *who should decide* what the police's priorities should be — whether they should concentrate on seat-belt offenders, catching burglars, or preventing breaches of the peace. Nor is this the only important area of police discretion: they also have wide scope in deciding *how* to enforce the law, whether to patrol in cars or on foot for example, which charges to bring, and whether to prosecute or caution suspects.

The police argue that they should be responsible for these decisions because of their accountability to the law, their professionalism, and their accountability to elected representatives and the public.

2. Accountability to the Law

Lord Denning has ruled, as we have seen, that a constable 'is not the servant of anyone save the law itself . . . the responsibility for law enforcement lies on him. He is answerable to the law and to the law alone'.[11]

The assertion that the police are accountable to the law means two things:

(a) that they have a duty to enforce the law, and
(b) that, in enforcing the law, they must act within the law.

(a) Duty to enforce the law

We have already seen that the police do not in fact consider that they have an *absolute* duty to enforce the law but rather a duty to do so selectively.

In chapter 2 we saw that the courts have consistently refused to challenge a chief constable's discretion, only intervening in extreme cases where he has not carried out his duty but never interfering with his discretion as to how to carry out that duty, provided that his actions are within the law.

The courts have been only a little less reluctant to penalise individual constables for failing to carry out their duty to enforce the law on the streets. In a rare case in 1981, the Court of Appeal upheld the conviction of a PC Dytham who witnessed a man being ejected from a night club and noisily kicked to death in the street but made no move to quell the disturbance or the attack. The court held that he had, without reasonable cause or justification, failed to carry out his duty to preserve the peace, protect the victim, and bring the assailant to justice.[12]

(b) Obligation to act within the law

We shall consider here the validity of the argument that the courts exercise control over police behaviour and that the police are thus accountable to the law. It must be remembered, however, that there is a distinction between control over the behaviour of individual officers and control over policing policy. Even if police officers were fully accountable to the courts for their individual actions (which, as we shall see, they are not), this would not undermine our argument that they are not accountable to the courts for policing policy — or for those areas of police work outside law enforcement.

To what extent does the law govern how the police do their job? What action can the courts take, for example, if a police officer does not follow the correct procedures laid down in the criminal law on the collection of evidence — or fails to observe the Judges' Rules on the treatment of suspects?

The answer is that the courts could, and should, provide one means of controlling the behaviour of individual officers. In many instances they do not, however, because: first, the wording of much of our legislation allows the police enormous discretion to decide when and how to act. Secondly, judges and magistrates are reluctant to question police behaviour. Thirdly, many of the rules governing police behaviour are not statutory at all, but simply guidelines.

The powers of arrest are one area where the law is confused. In the new Police and Criminal Evidence Act the government has now extended these powers to include, for example, minor offences such as dropping litter if the suspect refuses to give his/her address or the police do not believe them; or making an arrest to *prevent* an obstruction of the highway or indecent behaviour. It will be almost impossible to prove to a court that the police did not genuinely disbelieve the suspect when he/she give his/her name or address — or had no grounds for arresting someone to prevent an obstruction of the highway.

The Act also extends police powers to stop and search people if they have 'reasonable suspicion' that they are carrying stolen goods or an offensive weapon. Here again, the only recourse for the individual who has been stopped and searched without 'reasonable suspicion', or against whom the police have used unreasonable force, is to sue them for damages. They will then have to prove, often many years after the event, not merely that they were innocent but that the officer had no grounds for suspecting that they were guilty.[13]

The Judges' Rules and Administrative Directions which currently govern the treatment of suspects (e.g. their right to see a solicitor) are not statutory and are commonly ignored.[14] Many, such as the 'rule' that children under seventeen should not be questioned without a parent or guardian present, are not even grounds for civil action if breached, as they frequently are. These rules are incorporated into the Police Discipline Code; but, to take one example, the Metropolitan Police solicitor told NCCL that he could not remember when a member of that force had been disciplined for breaching any of the rules. An official enquiry in 1977 said of Administrative Direction 7, the right to see a solicitor, that it was unknown to the senior officers who gave evidence to the enquiry. 'In the Metropolitan Police District,' it concluded, 'it is not observed'.[15]

During a trial, the legal requirements regarding evidence should enable the judiciary to exercise control over police practices, but here too they have shown consistent reluctance to interfere in police discretion. In relation to evidence obtained as a result of illegal searches and arrests, for example, the House of Lords has ruled that 'It is no part of a judge's function to exercise disciplinary powers over the police or prosecution as respects the way in which evidence to be used at the trial is obtained by them'. If it was obtained illegally, Lord Diplock said,

> ... there will be a remedy in civil law; if it was obtained legally, but in breach of the rules of conduct for the police, this is a disciplinary matter ... However much the judge may dislike the way in which a particular piece of evidence was obtained before proceedings were commenced, if it is admissible evidence probative of the accused's guilt, it is no part of his judicial function to exclude it.[16]

A police officer who breaks the law can of course be prosecuted like any other citizen, a course of action which can be initiated by an official complaint by a member of the public, if the substance of the complaint constitutes a criminal offence. Alternatively, if the officer is found to have breached the Police Discipline Code, he can be disciplined by his/her chief officer. The Discipline Code and the complaints system are both the subject of much criticism, but beyond the scope of this book.[17]

The courts could provide more effective control over police use of their powers if two essential changes were made: first, laws allowing the police too great discretion should be tightened up (e.g. sections of the Public Order Act 1936) or repealed (e.g. stop-and-search powers). Secondly, the Judges' Rules should be made legally binding, any evidence obtained by the police in breach of the rules being automatically excluded from any subsequent trial.

There are, in addition, many areas of police work which do not come under judicial scrutiny at all. Within the area of law enforcement, the laws do not say *how* they should be enforced, whether, for example, by setting up special anti-crime squads or using home-beat patrols. Nor can the courts supervise those areas of police work which are not concerned with law enforcement, such as work in schools and crime prevention. When decisions have to be made concerning these aspects of their work, the police argue that we must rely on their 'professional judgement'.

3. Professional Judgement of the Police

Police authorities should remember, a chief constable said recently, that a chief constable is a qualified and experienced man who has learned from years of actual operational involvement, coupled with a high degree of training. 'He is as much qualified as the doctor, the dentist, the lawyer or any other professional — and no layman would think of interfering with the jobs of those people as they appear to wish to do with the police'.[18]

The police notion of professional judgement is very closely linked with that of impartiality: because of their 'professionalism' they are able to stand apart from prejudices and political bias and make decisions in the interests of the community as a whole. What is being developed, through the image of 'the professionals', is the view that the police 'are just as capable as doctors or lawyers or any other profession of self-regulation. Professionalism carries the potential for reduction in democratic or judicial control. It provides an alternative — and to the force a more acceptable — means of regulation than external control'.[19]

When we look at the views actually expressed by police officers, however, we find that, far from being above politics, they have strong political views which colour their perception of their role and priorities. Sir Robert Mark, for instance, a former Metropolitan Commissioner, has linked the problems the police face directly with socialism, arguing that the police are 'very much on their own in attempting to preserve order in an increasingly turbulent society in which socialist philosophy has changed from raising the standards of the poor and deprived to reducing the standards of the wealthy, the skilled and the deserving to the lowest common denominator'.[20] Justifying the use of police surveillance techniques, he continues: 'The simple truth is that fascists, communists, Trotskyites, anarchists *et al.* are committed to the overthrow of democracy and to the principle that the end justifies the means. Democracy must therefore protect itself by keeping a careful eye on them'.[21]

In another context, but equally revealing, John Alderson, then Chief Constable of Devon and Cornwall, and a strong advocate of police involvement in schools, blamed teachers for teaching children 'to challenge the statements of their elders, to expose the ignorance of their parents, to demand the source of the policeman's authority, to question the control of the employer, and even to show people how to go on strike . . .' Now, he said, 'We ask for the same energy and dedication towards new social control and containment of excessive and unacceptable behaviour'.[22]

It is not only the senior officers who express political views. In March 1982, the Police Federation launched a major law and order campaign to persuade Parliament to bring back the death penalty, reportedly paying £30,000 to place advertisements in five national newspapers.[23] Nor is it only such clear-cut political views which influence the police officer's judgement. Just as some officers have been found to feel more strongly about the seat-belt law than others, so their values inevitably affect all their decisions. Thus, their views of women in marriage may affect their willingness to take action against husbands who assault their wives, while their attitude to demonstrators or trade unionists may influence the way they police a demonstration or a picket line. The police undoubtedly have an expertise developed through their training and experience; but this does not mean that the decisions they take are based solely on technical, non-value-laden criteria, any more than those of other professionals such as teachers and social workers. Jack Straw MP took up this point when he argued:

> The special nature of police work means that they must have wide areas of independent professional discretion in relation to particular operations or cases. But the argument that this should entitle the police to immunity from any effective democratic accountability is as unconvincing today as it was when the Royal Commission reported. The conflict which exists between professional expertise and lay judgement, which exists elsewhere within any democratic system of government, is a healthy one — and generally produces a higher quality and more stable series of decisions.[24]

4. Accountability to Elected Representatives

The police do not always deny that their values influence their judgement but they then fall back on other safeguards to defend the status quo: just as police authorities, if given the power to control policing policy, would be bound to have prejudices and priorities, *Police* magazine has suggested, 'So it may be argued of chief constables. But they are accountable to the Home Secretary,

Parliament and the Courts'.[25]

We have already shown in chapter 2 that these forms of accountability are inadequate, and no more need be said here. But there is one final argument which the police use to justify their independence: their accountability to the general public.

5. Accountability to the Public

'Real accountability,' James Anderton says, 'has little to do with police committees, county councils or even Parliament. It is a matter which lies *directly* between the police and all the people they serve'.[26]

This point of view cannot be dismissed lightly because it illustrates that, in emphasising their direct relationship of accountability to the public, the police are relying on a very different meaning of the term 'accountability' from the one we have been using, to provide authority for their actions. To the police, accountability to the public apparently means two things: enforcing the law in the interests of the public as a whole, and thus earning their consent and support; and, second, giving an account of their actions afterwards to the public and its elected representatives. Thus Sir Robert Mark was perfectly sincere in his belief that 'The fact that the British police are answerable to the law, *that we act on behalf of the community* and not under the mantle of government, makes us the least powerful, the most accountable and therefore the most acceptable police in the world' (our emphasis).[27]

The police believe that they are better placed than elected representatives to balance sectional interests and decide what action would be in the interests of the public as a whole, many welcoming consultation with the public as a means of ascertaining what the public feel their interests are. Hence the strong link in police philosophy between consultation and accountability. Sir Kenneth Newman has said (quoting Lord Scarman):

> . . . accountability is a requirement for effective policing *and forms of consultation have to be evolved* which will 'ensure that the police in their policies and operations keep in touch with and are responsible to the community they police' [our emphasis].[28]

He noted as a promising development, which might help the police 'to be accountable without losing their independence', the growing use of public opinion surveys to obtain information on such things as the public's fears about crime or their perceptions of the quality of the police service.

The police appear to consider that, if they are acting in the interests of the whole community, and giving the public and their elected representatives (some) information about what they are doing, then they are 'accountable'. This belief is important because it underpins their understanding of the term 'policing by consent'. Conservative MP John Wheeler was expressing this view when he said, in a Commons debate on the Metropolitan Police, that if public co-operation were withdrawn from the police for any reason the police would be helpless and cease to function. 'That', he said, 'is the finest form of police accountability and it is far better than a police committee of politically motivated councillors'.[29]

Because public consent is such an important source of their authority, some senior officers have recently sought not only to ascertain public opinion but to create it, both through increasing use of the media and through participation in schools and youth activities. As Sir Robert Mark has explained, 'the post-war years have seen a gradual change in our role from mere law enforcement to participants in the role of social welfare and even more importantly to that of contributors in the moulding of public opinion and legislation'.[30]

Martin Kettle has described this development, which began with Sir Robert Mark's new 'open' approach to the media, and his conscious attempts to use it to press for change in the law and in policy (as in his controversial Dimbleby Lecture); the Police Federation's 'law and order' campaigns provide another example.[31] Always, Kettle points out, the police view is presented as the public's view, the Federation's campaign being 'to harness the public's growing concern about the state of crime and public order in Britain into a programme of positive action'. He describes also the Metropolitan Police's decision to introduce press credentials selectively and Sir Robert Mark's arrangement with the BBC over coverage of 'delicate' issues.

Increasingly, Kettle shows, the police claim to speak on behalf of society as a whole, just as they believe they are acting on behalf of a society in consensus. Whatever they decide becomes, by definition, in the interests of law and order and thus of 'society' too. Whoever opposes them is thus, equally by definition, hostile to law and order and therefore to society.

The decision by the Metropolitan Police in 1982 to publish statistics purporting to show that black people were disproportionately involved in 'mugging' is one illustration of their attempts to manufacture public opinion — in this case to undermine the Scarman Report which had recommended more sensitive policing of ethnic minority areas, a recommendation some officers apparently interpreted as 'go soft on the blacks'.

The police argued that they released the statistics in response to public pressure for the facts. When asked *how* they tapped public opinion, they referred to the media. But an examination of recent media coverage of 'muggings' showed, according to Gareth Pierce, a solicitor writing in *The Guardian*, that the concern in this instance was generated by the police themselves.[32] The police are of course entitled to hold opinions and to promote them, but it is not legitimate for them to create media coverage and then point to it as evidence of public concern. As Stuart Hall puts it, 'First forming public opinion; then, disingenuously, consulting it'.

Hall argues that the police cannot both constitute a powerful crusading part of the 'law and order' lobby and maintain their appearance of impartiality. 'They cannot claim to "police by consent" and be so actively and publicly involved in constructing public opinion, in shaping consent and producing it, in its most traditionalist and disciplinary form'.[33]

A central weakness of the assertion that the police are accountable to the public because they police with their consent is that this consent is so clearly lacking in some sections of the public. The disturbances of 1981, the reaction to such incidents as the death of Colin Roach in a London police station in January 1983, and even some opinion polls, all provide evidence of this lack of consent.

It is clear, moreover, that the relationship which the police seek with the public is not actually one of 'accountability' at all. It relies on the public having a passive role, perhaps coming forward to 'consult' or provide information, but leaving it to the police to identify their views and measure their consent. If the police attempt to manufacture that consent, their position has even less legitimacy. If they fail and that consent is lost in certain sections of the community, the police cannot, under this informal system, actually be called to account.

Preserving the Existing Structure

It is because none of these forms of accountability is in fact adequate that public frustration at their inability to influence policing has grown, and with it demands for new forms of accountability which will be effective. Recognising that public confidence in the police has declined in some areas, and faced with increasing demands for greater accountability, those who wish to preserve police independence have put forward two of their own proposals in an attempt to prop up the existing structure: first, that police authorities should demonstrate the potential of their existing powers, without interfering with the independence of the police in operational matters, and, second, that a network of police-public consultative committees should be established.

While it is arguable that both these proposals can also be used by those pressing for genuine accountability, this is not necessarily the intention of their promoters.

(a) Activating police authorities

The first objective has been most clearly articulated in a pamphlet published by the Social Affairs Unit entitled 'Are the Police Under Control?' Its author, David Regan, is Professor of Local Government at Nottingham University.[34]

The purpose of the pamphlet, Regan writes, is to urge police committees to adopt 'a more active and involved stance but *within* the existing system' (his emphasis). He begins by citing the 1981 disturbances and noting that the key issue they raised, both for those who thought that the police had been over-cautious in their reaction and for those who thought they had over-reacted, was 'Who controls the police?'

Regan then explains the role which police authorities are supposed to play and notes the criticism of them as ineffective. He feels, however, that there would be dangers in introducing new legislation to increase their powers. 'What is perceived as an imbalance may be *over*-corrected', and such a danger should be avoided. Central to his argument is his belief that police independence must be protected. 'At its best', he writes, 'it can be the equivalent of the doctor's Hippocratic oath' — although he acknowledges that it can be taken too far. However it is 'too precious to be squandered on needless conflicts with police committees'.

Regan reviews the role which police authorities are playing, criticising their tendency to rubber-stamp most decisions while over-reacting to the less important, such as a proposal to buy foreign cars. At one point he accuses them of intellectual sloth, but he has no criticisms of the extent of their existing powers.

The gist of his recommendations is that they must begin to use their powers — to ask for reports, to scrutinise establishment figures and the handling of complaints — and he concludes that by so doing they 'could achieve much general influence over their force, whatever the legal niceties'. The indications are, he writes, that many chief constables would respond positively to informed and sensible initiatives from their authorities.

The philosophy behind his recommendations is revealed when he advises police authorities on how to deal with recalcitrant chief constables. It must be explained to them, he writes, that having more informed and influential police committees is, in the long run, advantageous to the police themselves, even if in the short run it makes life more difficult for them:

> The public concern about control of the police has already been stressed. There is a danger of a polarisation of public opinion developing which would undermine the whole tradition of policing by consent — then life really would be made difficult for the police. *An alliance between police committees and chief constables would help to defuse this situation* [our emphasis].[35]

Giving a public lecture in 1980, Mr Whitelaw, then Home Secretary, argued in a similar vein:

> I do not take the view that there is any case for major changes in the organisation of the police. The present arrangements . . . achieve on the whole a satisfactory balance between local, operational and central interests . . .
>
> That does not mean, however, that I see no scope for movement and development within the existing statutory framework . . . I think it has become increasingly desirable that police authorities should see themselves not just as providers of resources but as a means whereby the chief constable can give account of his policing policy to the democratically elected representatives of the community and, in turn, they can express to him the views of the community on these policies. I believe that many police authorities already take this view of their role. I also believe that it is not something for which one can legislate but which must grow out of a relationship of mutual trust and confidence between a police authority and its chief constable . . . Developments on these lines would, I believe, do much to ensure that police forces adapt sensitively to meet the needs of the communities they serve.[36]

The government itself has said little formally on these lines, perhaps because some of the authorities which are exercising their responsibilities are not so emphatic about the need to respect the limits of their powers. The position the present government has adopted is to encourage the establishment of a network of consultative committees throughout the country, a proposal it encouraged initially by circular in 1982 and then reiterated in a weaker form in its Police and Criminal Evidence Act.

(b) Establishing consultative committees

On 16 June 1982, the Home Office published guidelines for local consultation/liaison arrangements between police and community representatives.[37] Lord Scarman had recommended that a statutory duty be imposed on police authorities and chief constables to co-operate in setting up consultative arrangements, but at this stage the Home Secretary was still considering whether the arrangements for consulting the public should be given statutory force.[38] In the event, the Police and Criminal Evidence Act makes provision only for 'arrangements' in which the police would not be obliged to co-operate and which need not necessarily be interpreted to mean a consultative group meeting regularly, as the guidelines had proposed.

Lord Scarman also recommended that the Home Secretary remain the police authority for the Metropolitan Police and that a framework for consultation between the police and community representatives be established at *borough* level, thus effectively by-passing the Greater London Council and its Police Committee, a recommendation also readily adopted in the guidelines.

The guidelines stress that the new committees are for consultation only and will not affect the independence of the police in enforcing the law. The purposes of consultation are to enable the police to adapt their policies to meet the community's needs; to improve police-community relations; to promote agreed solutions to local problems, and to provide opportunities for the community to gain a better understanding of the police.

The size and membership of the committees, and the area covered (e.g. one police district or the whole force), are to be local decisions. (It is unclear whether the police authority/London borough and the police would make the decisions or whether community representatives would have a say — and if so, who.) The guidelines also leave open whether or not meetings should be open to the public.

The guidelines suggest that MPs and local councillors should be on the committee as well as representatives of government departments such as the NHS, DOE and DES and local government departments like social services. Other suggestions include CRCs, trades councils, chambers of commerce, magistrates, ethnic minority organisations, churches and councils for voluntary service. (NB: law centres, local solicitors and citizens advice bureaux are obvious omisions.) One London borough, Hillingdon, quickly decided to exclude its local CRC.

General suggestions are made on the kind of issues which could be discussed — 'issues of local concern', joint crime prevention exercises, creation of opportunities for the community to gain a better understanding of the police and *vice versa*, and 'policing responses to crime problems, in particular responses which may affect relations with the community'.

They do not exclude 'operational matters' from discussion but do stress that the community should understand the limitations of consultation. Consultative groups cannot intervene in the enforcement of the criminal law:

> *therefore the deployment of officers, the method and timing of police operations and the stage at which these may be discussed*, are matters for the chief constable/commissioner and his officers ... nor can consultative groups be the forum for pursuit of individual cases which may be under investigation or *sub judice*; nor for the discussion of allegations of crime or of individual complaints against police officers for which formal procedures already exist.
>
> ... Within these well established limits, issues directly or indirectly concerned with the policing of the local community ... may be considered *so that the decisions which are properly for the police or the police authority/Home Secretary can be more closely informed* by the discussion of local needs [our emphasis].

To counter criticisms that earlier liaison committees had been dominated by the police, the guidelines say that meetings will not normally be chaired by the police; in London, the Metropolitan Police 'do not wish to be considered for the chairmanship of such groups'.

Notes of the main points raised at the meetings should be sent to the police authority and the chief constable, to be taken into account in their discussions about policing of the force area as a whole. In London, they are to be sent to the Commissioner for his discussions with the Home Secretary (NB: not directly to the Home Secretary, as the police authority). Members of the committees may relate the *conclusions* of the discussions to members of the public.

The government's guidelines did not even go as far as the terms of reference of the Lambeth Consultative Group established by the Home Secretary after the disturbances in 1981. The terms of reference of this group begin: 'The committee may consider and discuss any matters directly or indirectly concerned with the policing of Lambeth' and specifically state that 'the Police Commander *will* consult the consultative group on general matters of policy relating to policing and operations in Lambeth (recognising that the final decision rests with the Commander)' and that 'save in exceptional cases the Police Commander will give prior notice of his intention to mount major operations'. Where notice could not be given in advance 'the Police Commander may be *required* to account retrospectively to the Consultative Group for the particular type of operation mounted' (our emphasis).

The Lambeth group was also to be open to any *bona fide* local organisation representing a significant section of the community provided it supported the group's aims. The failure of the guidelines to use the Lambeth terms of reference as their model, despite the previous Home Secretary's assurance that the group was 'a model of what the Bill would require',[39] has led to criticism from bodies such as the London Association of Community Relations Councils (LACRC), which would have been prepared to participate in such committees had the Lambeth criteria been adopted throughout London.[40]

A survey conducted by LACRC in February 1984 revealed that, of the twenty-two boroughs which had established consultative committees, only three had explicitly agreed that police operations could be discussed. Twelve did not discuss operations and in seven the position was unclear. Of the twelve which did not discuss operations, six had terms of reference which explicitly excluded such discussion. Eighteen of the committees, like Lambeth, operated an 'open door' policy to *bona fide* local organisations but seven did not. A survey published in June 1984 showed that all but six of the forty-three forces in England and Wales had set up some form of consultative committee.[41]

The Role of Liaison Committees

In order to assess the role of these committees it is important to remember the distinction between *accountability* and *consultation*: the police are accountable to a committee if they are *obliged* to inform that committee about their activities *and* the committee can apply some sanction against the officers responsible if it does not approve of their actions.

Consultation between the police and that committee, however, means only that the police listen to the committee's views and vice versa. There is no obligation on either side to act on what the other has said. Consultation is not, therefore, a form of accountability. Under such arrangements, the police are not obliged to tell the committee anything, and if committee members do not like what they are told they are powerless to do anything about it.

The Home Secretary's guidelines and the proposals in the new Act make it clear that the proposed liaison committees are for consultation only and are not intended to enhance police accountability. The question we may ask, therefore, is whether the existence of a network of such committees would:

(a) Effect any improvement in policing policies and practices despite the fact that the public cannot oblige the police to change.
(b) Form a positive half-way step towards greater accountability — or, alternatively, prove counter-productive in that campaign.

(a) Would liaison committees bring about improvements in policing?

Past experience of liaison committees suggests that consultation does not give the public greater influence over the policing of their area. As we have seen, on one occasion in Lambeth the commander failed even to inform the liaison committee of his intention to bring in the special patrol group for a major and controversial operation. Early in 1982, members of the newly established prototype consultative committee in Lambeth complained that the commander had failed to inform them about 'Operation Streetwise', an operation significant enough to be launched at a public meeting in Lambeth Town Hall. Members of similar committees have complained that the police are unwilling to discuss controversial issues or to allow the committee to influence their work. Their frustration is an inevitable outcome of a consultation process in which the police do not have to take the committee's views into account.

The liaison committees which are now being established differ in no significant way from their predecessors and the experience of those who participate is unlikely to be any different. Although well-intentioned chief officers will prove flexible on certain issues, they will guard their independence jealously and want to be seen to do so.

The existence of such committees (members of which are non-elected and thus accountable to no one) could indeed prove a detriment to policing standards, if police chiefs use the support of an acquiescent committee to legitimise otherwise unacceptable policing methods.

(b) Would they be a useful half-way step towards accountability?

There is no suggestion in the government's proposals nor in Scarman's recommendations that the liaison committee could or should ever develop beyond consultation. The proposals to offer consultation must unfortunately be seen as an attempt to appease increasing demands for accountability by offering a palliative which neither increases community control nor weakens police autonomy.

The long-term effect of the establishment of a network of liaison committees could in fact be to divert attention and pressure from the campaign for accountability. They could raise the hopes of some sections of the community that real changes can be achieved, thus discouraging them from participation in alternative initiatives. Moreover, the existence of such a network will encourage the police and the government to claim, because of the confusion between 'accountability' and 'consultation', that the police *are* accountable and to reject demands for greater statutory powers for police authorities.

The existence of non-elected liaison committees could undermine the authority of the elected bodies and marginalise their role, despite the fact that it is the police authority which has the statutory responsibility for the efficiency of the force. Police authority members may find that issues of local concern are increasingly being discussed at liaison meetings rather than by the authority. Chief constables could use the views of the liaison committee to undermine police authority decisions, although liaison committee members are non-elected and not necessarily representative of the community's views. In London, a network of borough-based liaison committees would reinforce the position of the Home Secretary as police authority for the Metropolitan Police, undermining the demand by the GLC to be given a say in the policing of London as a whole.

Liaison committees are thus not intended to be a step towards accountability — nor will they achieve that effect. On the contrary, the existence of such committees could be counter-productive if it undermines the campaign for genuine accountability and enables the government to postpone the legislative changes that are long overdue.

In NCCL's view it does not follow that local groups should therefore refuse to participate in a consultative committee if such a body is set up in their area. Once the committee is in existence there may be strong arguments in favour of participation and against abstention, depending on the local political situation.[42]

Notes

1. James Anderton, 'The Reality of Community Policing', in *Police and Society Research Papers* Vol.1 No.5 (August 1982).

2. *Police* (August 1980).
3. *Police Regulations* 1971.
4. House of Commons Disqualification Act 1975, s.1.
5. Sir Kenneth Newman, 'Police Policy and Crime Control', Fifth Cranfield Conference (June 1982).
6. Lord Scarman, *The Brixton Disorders 10-12 April 1981*, Cmnd 8427, para.4.58.
7. Sir Kenneth Newman, *op.cit.*
8. *The Guardian*, 21 January 1983.
9. *Sunday Times*, 30 January 1983.
10. Home Affairs Committee Report, *Race Relations and the 'Sus' Law* (House of Commons, April 1980), HC 559.
11. Lord Denning in *R* v. *Metropolitan Police Commissioner* ex parte *Blackburn* [1968] 2 QB 118.
12. *Police Review*, 19 June 1981.
13. See *Rights*, Vol.7 No.1, a special issue on the Police and Criminal Evidence Bill.
14. The Judges' Rules and Administrative Directions are to be replaced by a Code of Practice under the Police and Criminal Evidence Act but will remain non-statutory.
15. *Report of an Inquiry by the Hon. Sir Henry Fisher into the circumstances leading to the trial of three persons on charges arising out of the death of Maxwell Confait and the fire at 27 Doggett Rd, London SE6* (HMSO, 1977), para.2.17(d).
16. *R* v. *Sang* [1980]AC (H.L.(E)), as per Lord Diplock pp.436-7.
17. See Patricia Hewitt, *A Fair Cop: Reforming the Police Complaints Procedure* (NCCL, 1982).
18. Barry Pain, Chief Constable of Kent and President of ACPO, to the Joint Conference of ACPO, ACC and AMA. *The Guardian*, 9 June 1982.
19. Doreen McBarnet, 'The Royal Commission and the Judges' Rules', *British Journal of Law and Society*, Vol.8, No.1 (summer 1981), pp.115-16.
20. Robert Mark, *In the Office of Constable* (Fontana, 1979), p.259.
21. *Ibid.*, p.311.
22. *The Guardian*, 7 September 1978.
23. *The Guardian*, 18 March 1982.
24. Jack Straw, MP, 'Memorandum on the Police Authorities Powers Bill' (November 1979).
25. *Police* (August 1980).
26. James Anderton, *op.cit.*
27. Robert Mark, *op.cit.*, p.149.
28. Sir Kenneth Newman, *op.cit.*, p.14.
29. *Hansard*, 28 February 1983.
30. Introduction to T.A. Critchley, *A History of Police in England and Wales* (Constable, revised edition 1978), p.xiii.
31. Martin Kettle, 'The Politics of Policing and the Policing of Politics', in Peter Hain (ed.), *Policing the Police*, Vol.2 (John Calder, 1980).
32. *The Guardian*, 15 March 1982.
33. Stuart Hall, *Drifting into a Law and Order Society* (Cobden Trust, 1979).
34. David Regan, 'Are the Police Under Control?' (Social Affairs Unit, 1983).
35. *Ibid.*, p.12.
36. The James Smart Lecture, Edinburgh, 17 September 1980.
37. Circular 54/1982. The Home Office has subsequently issued a further set of draft guidelines for London, under the Police and Criminal Evidence Bill: *'Draft guidance on arrangements for local consultation between the community and the police in the Metropolitan Police District 15 March 1984'.*

38. *Hansard*, 16 June 1982.
39. *Hansard*, 5 November 1982, col.225.
40. See, for example, LACRC briefings to MPs on the 1983 and 1984 Police and Criminal Evidence Bill and its *London Agenda* (1982).
41. LACRC, 'Community/Police Consultation: Summary of the London Boroughs Arrangements' (February 1984, unpublished); also Rod Morgan and Christopher Maggs *Following Scarman?* (Centre for the Analysis of Social Policy, Bath University, June 1984).
42. NCCL policy paper 'Participation in Police/Community Consultative Committees' (November 1984).

CHAPTER 5
Proposals for Reform

We stated in the introduction to this book our commitment to the principle that individuals who are elected or appointed to exercise power over others should be accountable for their actions. We suggested that an examination of the respective powers of the police and of the elected representatives to whom they are said to be accountable would demonstrate that this principle is not upheld by the present system of police accountability in England and Wales.

In chapters 2 and 3 we showed that the 1964 Police Act was not intended to place chief constables under the control of elected representatives; nor did it make the police accountable to these representatives, police authorities having been given no powers either to instruct chief constables or to reprimand them if they do not observe the authorities' guidelines. The powers of police authorities, we saw, are circumscribed both by those of their chief constables and by those of the Home Secretary.

The police are, to a certain extent, accountable to the law. This means of accountability is often ineffective in practice, however, the courts rarely choosing to intervene. It also covers only certain aspects of police work excluding, crucially, police discretion over *how* they enforce the law. In London, we saw that the absence of accountability is particularly acute.

In chapter 4 we demonstrated the weaknesses of the arguments used to defend the status quo and the limitations of the proposals for change put forward by those seeking to protect the police from democratic control.

In making the case for democratic control we are not only seeking to defend a principle. The effect of police autonomy has been demonstrated clearly in periodic public concern and criticism of police priorities, policies and methods of crime prevention and law enforcement. The consequent alienation of sections of the public has reduced public co-operation with the police and hence their effectiveness. There have been many indications of public frustration at their inability to influence the policing of their area because of the lack of any form of genuine democratic control.

NCCL believes that this situation could be remedied only by a radical transformation of the constitutional position of the police to enable democratically elected representatives to determine police policies, priorities and policing methods within the law: to create a *genuine* tripartite structure in which the authority of police authorities, and of Parliament, is real and effective. It is our contention that *locally* elected representatives should, to a significant extent, determine the priorities, policies and policing methods of their local force and the resources to be devoted to them. In order to balance these powers, however, it is essential that there should be a framework of national guidelines and standards on policing methods and equipment agreed by our nationally elected representatives in Parliament. Within these constraints locally elected representatives (in a reconstructed police authority) would be expected to ensure, as in other areas of local government, that the policies and priorities of the police reflected the concerns of their communities.

This proposal goes further than most existing arguments for reform. This is because the belief that the police must remain independent of democratic control if they are to remain impartial (accompanied by constant reassurances that they are nevertheless accountable to the law instead) has had a major impact on the form that proposals for change have taken.

Early Proposals for Reform

Although accountability to the law can only, as we have seen, be said to apply to those decisions supervised by the courts — i.e., those relating to law enforcement — the police have successfully argued that they must in fact be independent in all 'operational' matters, a wider term which is used to encompass all decisions relating to police operations, including, for example, crime prevention. Although the term 'operational' does not appear in the 1964 Police Act nor in the relevant court judgements, it is used to justify police autonomy in a wider range of decisions than the case law would appear to support. Thus Mr Whitelaw, when Home Secretary, stated:

> I think most people in this country would agree that it is highly desirable that the enforcement of the criminal law should not be subjected to political control or influence. As Home Secretary, I cannot give directions to chief constables on *operational* matters and neither can police authorities.[1]

Similarly, South Yorkshire Police Authority, in its report on its enquiry into relations between the police and the public, was anxious to put on record that 'at no time was the motive for setting up the working party a desire to interfere with operational matters'.[2]

This adherence to the notion of autonomy in operational matters has led to an untenable distinction being made between operational decisions (to be left to the police), and policy decisions (in which, it is generally accepted, the public or their elected representatives may legitimately have some say). Policing 'policy' appears to cover such matters as the distribution of resources and manpower (e.g. to districts and special squads), levels of equipment, priorities of the force and so on, but not, for example, the planning of a particular investigation, which would be an 'operational' matter. Clearly, the distinction is a difficult one to make because all operational decisions are, or should be, the product of policy and policy decisions are, in part, made as a result of operational experience. 'Operation Swamp' in 1981 was the result of a policy decision to tackle the street crime in Brixton by saturation policing methods. The disastrous consequences of that operation, in the civil disturbances in April, had implications for revising future policy and hence future operations.

Despite the obviously close inter-relation between policy and operational decisions, some advocates of reform have attempted to maintain a clear distinction, advocating democratic control over policy but leaving operational decisions to the police.

(i) The Straw Bills

On 14 November 1979 Jack Straw, MP for Blackburn, used the 'Ten-Minute Rule' procedure to introduce his Police Authorities (Powers) Bill in the House of Commons to give police authorities the power to decide the 'general policing policies' for their area. In March 1980 he introduced a second Bill to:

1. create a locally elected police authority for London's police;
2. extend the powers of police authorities on similar lines to his previous Bill:
3. remove magistrates from police authorities;
4. create a National Police Agency responsible for the Metropolitan Police's national functions, and
5. permit police authorities to see the reports of the Inspectorate of Constabulary.

The parliamentary procedure relating to Private Members Bills ensured that neither Bill got very far; but they did succeed in putting the idea of such reforms on the political agenda.

Giving the authorities the power to determine general policing policies, Straw said, would enable them to decide, for instance, whether policemen should be put back on the beat and to issue instructions to their chief constables accordingly. However, in order to protect the chief constables' independence over deployment in particular cases and situations, Straw's initial Bill gave the chief constable the power to (a) delay implementation of an authority's decision for six months and/or (b) appeal to the Home Secretary if he felt that the authority had overstepped its powers. The Bill also gave the authority the power to seek information from the chief constable on operational and organisational matters — subject to safeguards on disclosure of information relating to investigations, and to personal and security matters. The Bill also increased the authorities' powers in relation to the complaints procedure and extended their powers of appointment down to the level of superintendent. Straw made it quite clear that:

> . . . my Bill specifically safeguards, through appeal to the Home Secretary, the necessary day-to-day operational independence of the chief constable.[3]

> . . . it is no part of the intention behind this Bill that elected members of police committees should become involved in decisions on particular cases, either as to the deployment of the police, or to the decisions on prosecutions.[4]

Straw's proposals, which would allow the police to retain control of operational matters, only having a duty to provide information about them, clearly would not overcome the problems of the present system. To take the example of Brixton: if a London police authority had had the powers Straw proposed, it could have given general policy directions — that more men should be on the beat, for example, and (arguably) that the SPG should not be used — and after Operation Swamp it could have asked for information about it. But without any control over the operation itself, or any sanction to apply to the officers (whose judgement, in setting up Operation Swamp, Scarman considered a 'serious mistake'), the authority would have no power to reprimand those responsible so as to ensure that it did not happen again. Although the police authority could argue that the use of saturation stop-and-search methods was a *policy* decision and forbid the use of such methods, the police could argue that this was an *operational* decision (deadlock) — or even that they could not fulfil their duty to enforce the law against street crime without resorting to such methods — and thus overrule the police authority.

(ii) The Association of Metropolitan Authorities (AMA)

Some fourteen months after Jack Straw introduced his second Bill, the county council elections of May 1981 resulted in the election of a number of Labour-controlled councils committed to extending their influence over their chief constables. Their police committees resolved not only to make more use of their existing powers but in some cases to press for more powers and for the removal of the non-elected magistrates from the authority.

The first meeting of the new Manchester Police Authority, for instance, resolved to call on the AMA to press for the removal of magistrates; for a redefinition of the strategic responsibility of the authority for the policing of its area; and for an extension of the authority's powers of appointment.[5]

The AMA, which represents local authorities in metropolitan areas, responded by setting up a series of working parties on different aspects of policing, including accountability, the reports of which were published in November 1982 as 'Policies for the Police Service'.

The AMA proposals specifically endorse the Straw Bill, although their choice of wording is less specific, calling, as the Manchester Authority had suggested, for legislation to 'define more accurately the strategic responsibility of the police authority for the policing of its area'. In the meantime it called on the Home Secretary to issue guidelines 'which can form the basis of good practice to be followed by both police authorities and chief constables', a proposal the then Home Secretary accepted but never implemented.

Like Straw, the AMA called for the removal of non-elected magistrates, for an extension of the authority's powers of appointment to the rank of superintendent, for a locally elected police authority for London, for HMI reports to be made available to police authorities, and for national police services to be supervised by an independent body — in the case of the AMA this being comprised of Home Office and police authority representatives. The AMA also recommended that police authorities and chief constables should have a statutory duty to set up liaison committees 'to provide a forum in which police and community representatives can discuss local policing problems and other matters of mutual concern'.

The central weakness of the Straw and AMA proposals is that, while they enable the police authorities to determine police policy, they leave the police with complete control over operational decisions. They neither give the authorities the power to tell the police how to enforce the law nor the power to reprimand them after the event if their methods do not comply with the authority's policies. These proposals do not therefore make the police accountable for their operational decisions.

The question then arises: would it be sufficient and feasible to give the authorities direct control over policies, and to make the police genuinely accountable *after the event* for operational decisions? The authority would then lay down policy guidelines and be able to impose sanctions on the police after an operation if they did not observe these guidelines. The police would remain responsible for directing police operations, the authority having no power to instruct them in advance in relation to operational matters.

While this would appear on paper to give police authorities greater control over the police by making the police accountable to the authority for operational decisions, it simply would not be operable in practice because it relies on the untenable distinction between policy and operational decisions. Who is to decide what is a 'policy' decision and therefore open to police authority direction, and what is an 'operational' matter on which the police cannot be directed but for which they are accountable afterwards? It would be a recipe for conflict between police authorities and their forces, neither of which would know which decision fell within their control. If there is concern about transferring the direction of both policy *and* operational decisions to the police authority, it must be addressed by the introduction of alternative safeguards to restrict the scope of their powers.

In NCCL's view, it is necessary to give elected representatives the ultimate authority to direct the police on their policies, priorities *and* operational methods if elected representatives are effectively to determine, and be responsible for, the policing of our community; that is, if policing is to be brought within democratic control.

The police authority should, for instance, be able to determine, within any guidelines set by Parliament, the policing policies for its area — relating to both crime prevention and law enforcement — and to require its officers to implement these policies. If the authority believes that the priorities of its force should be changed and more resources devoted to, say, traffic control, or that more officers should be put on the beat, it should have the power to implement these changes. If certain policing methods are causing public concern, such as the use of special task forces, the authority should have the power, having consulted its police officers, to instruct the force to change its methods. Similarly, if a particular kind of criminal behaviour, perhaps vandalism or street robberies, requires additional police resources, the decision to redirect those resources should be that of the locally elected representatives, who know their area and are accountable to the electorate for their actions.

If authorities were to be given responsibility for policing they should, of course, have a statutory duty to enforce the law. A key question then remains: should the police also retain their statutory duty to enforce the law, or merely a duty delegated to them by the authority? The answer which is given to this question reflects the degree of control over operational decisions which it is felt the police should have.

Duty to Enforce the Law

The significance of the police retaining their statutory duty to enforce the law would be that they could use it to challenge any instructions from an authority which they considered prevented them from fulfilling that duty. If, for example, the authority instructed the police not to frequent public lavatories to enforce the law against homosexuals importuning, the police could argue that there was no other way in which they could enforce that law — a law democratically agreed by Parliament. If the police authority refused to withdraw the instruction, the police could challenge it in court. Similarly, they might argue that they could only fully enforce the law against theft by using stop-and-search methods; detect professional criminals by 'bugging' their telephones, or prevent a breach of the peace at a picket line by out-numbering the pickets.

In such disputes, the authority's judgement that the police *could* enforce the law in other ways would be pitted against the professional expertise of the police and the police authority might be unlikely to win. Would the police thus be able to challenge almost any policy with which they were in disagreement, thus undermining the control of the authority; or would their retention of their statutory duty to enforce the law in fact simply act as a necessary and desirable deterrent to prevent police authorities exceeding their powers?

If the police retained their statutory duty to enforce the law, a police authority would certainly not be able to instruct them not to enforce the law on any particular occasion. To do so would be to instruct them to neglect their statutory duty. At present, as we have seen, the police themselves regularly decide not to enforce the law because of the particular circumstances of the case or incident. But while they retain their statutory duty to enforce it, no police authority could instruct them not to, however tense the situation might be and however misguided the elected representatives might feel the police action to be.

If the police are using their discretion in this way, it could be argued that it should be exercised by elected representatives who are accountable to the public. Or would this enable the elected representatives, in practice, to instruct the police to neglect the law for their own reasons about which the public might be ill-informed and therefore unable to call them to account?

In short, if the authorities had ultimate responsibility for policy and operational matters but the police retained their statutory duty to enforce the law, the police would retain a considerable amount of direct control over their work. The safeguards (or limitations) of this proposal (depending on your point of view) are removed if the duty to enforce the law is simply delegated by the authority. The authority would then be able to instruct the police when to enforce the law and, in particular instances, not to enforce it at all. The authority, however, could be called to account in the courts for breaching its statutory duty.

The GLC Police Committee is the only official body to have proposed reforms which would give the authorities that degree of control. In its consultation paper 'A New Police Authority for London'[6] it gave the following example of a situation in which a police authority might choose to intervene to instruct the police not to enforce the law:

> A police authority might become aware that a corporate landlord in its area is proposing to evict squatters from a whole street of empty properties. There may be a general policy that the police should be present on such occasions only to ensure that there is no breach of the peace and that they should have as few police officers as possible visible. Subject to that, there may be delegated authority for senior police officers to assist on such an occasion without reference to the police authority. Nevertheless, the police authority may decide that this particular set of evictions is a different case, both because of public concern about the extent of likely opposition and because of its own local councillors' objections. It may be very worried about a widespread outbreak of public disorder inspired by large scale police involvement in such an event. It may therefore decide to recall its authority and instruct the police not to participate *on this occasion* [their emphasis].[7]

If this incident took place now, the police could, and well might, decide to have only a few officers present in order not to provoke public disorder by their presence. (This, indeed, was the approach Lord Scarman and the Metropolitan Commissioner recommended when they argued that the police should sometimes put the maintenance of order before law enforcement.) However, the elected representatives could *ensure* that they did this only if the police's statutory duty to enforce the law were transferred to the police authority. If the police retained their statutory duty to enforce the law they could *insist* on being present to enable them to do so. They would then still be subject to a dual accountability: to the law — which they would be required both to enforce and to obey; and to the police authority, for the way in which they enforced the law.

If a police authority had a statutory duty to enforce the law and failed to do so, the courts could intervene to oblige it to act. Although the courts have allowed the police wide discretion as to when they enforce the law, they can, in theory, force the police to do so when they fail to act. If the duty to enforce the law was transferred to police authorities, the courts might not allow them the same measure of discretion. Taking the GLC example of an authority instructing the police not to be present during the eviction of squatters, for example, the landlord of the property could ask the court to *instruct* the authority to carry out its duty to enforce the law — to prevent damage to his property, say, or a breach of the peace. Similarly, if an authority instructed the police not to interfere with the pickets outside a factory, the employer could ask the courts to instruct the authority to enforce the law to prevent obstruction of the gateway. Police authorities might thus find their discretion fettered by the courts to a far greater extent than the police have done.

Doubts and Criticisms

There are a number of doubts which can immediately be raised about a proposal to give elected representatives direction of the police, irrespective of which body has the duty to enforce the law.

(i) It would put the police under 'political control'

This is the first criticism which is made of any proposal to give authorities these powers. The criticism arises from the assumption that the police are now independent and impartial and that to put them under the control of elected representatives would result in biased policing, possibly directed against particular groups or individuals. In fact, as we have seen, police officers are not impartial, their exercise of discretion being influenced by many factors including force orders devised by senior officers, and their own values and prejudices. The question is whether their discretion should continue to be under the political control of a small group of senior officers and Home Office officials or under the political control of those who have been elected to represent the views of the public.

(ii) A police authority would be able to overrule Parliament

A second criticism concerns the respective powers of central and local government. Assuming that the duty to enforce the law were transferred to the police authority, would not an authority which instructed the police not to enforce the law be overruling a higher authority — that of Parliament, which passed the law?

The authority would be overruling Parliament if it instructed the police *never* to enforce a particular law — but it would not be allowed to do this because either the authority or the police, or both, would have a statutory duty to enforce the law. The situation now is that, although the police have a duty to enforce the law, they choose not to enforce it on certain occasions, whether because of a shortage of resources or the insignificance of the crime, or because to do so would aggravate an already tense situation. Neither the authority nor the police could overrule Parliament by rejecting a particular law altogether.

(iii) It would be impractical for a police authority to exercise operational control

It may also be argued that it would be impractical for a committee to be responsible for deploying officers on the street. It could not, for example, be consulted before officers acted in an emergency.

This problem would be overcome, as in all other areas of public service, by the authority delegating its powers to its officers, and making provision for decisions to be taken in an emergency, while retaining ultimate authority. The advantage of this system is that, *if* a situation did arise when the authority felt it appropriate, it could intervene. Most policing decisions would continue to be made by the professionals on the ground, but these decisions would be made under a delegated authority which could be recalled, limited or extended at any time. As the GLC argues, such a reform would not mean that the police would be subject to continuous interference by members of the authority in professional matters: 'As with other branches of local government activity, the police would have wide scope to exercise their discretion within the limits laid down by statute and according to police authority priorities. Control of operational matters would not mean the supervision of every detail'.[8]

As the GLC argues, giving the police authority ultimate responsibility for policing would not mean any diminution in the professional status of a police officer or in the importance attached to his/her judgement. There is a direct comparison here, they suggest, with the control exercised by local authorities over their employees — social workers, environmental health officers, housing managers, and so on: 'When a local authority changes its political complexion, its officers do not change and their duties remain broadly the same as before. Priorities or emphasis in the carrying out of those duties may change under different political control, but the basic tasks remain the same'.[9]

Moreover, the GLC points out, some local government officers have, like the police, statutory duties to carry out. When a social worker makes a place of safety order, for example, he/she uses his/her professional judgement and must also act within the law, i.e. he/she will only make the order if satisfied that there are grounds under the Children and Young Persons Act 1969 to do so. Similarly, a police officer cannot make an arrest unless he/she has reasonable grounds to suspect the person he/she is arresting of an arrestable offence.

(iv) Authorities might make unpopular decisions

Is there not a danger that many authorities would make decisions with which many members of the public would disagree? The answer to this question is certainly yes: even decisions which are agreed democratically will not meet everyone's approval. But these decisions are now being made by a small group of non-elected men in secret, and would at least become the responsibility of an elected body, accountable to the electorate, holding its meetings in public.

(v) Too much power would be concentrated in the police authority

There is a further criticism which has to be considered very carefully: if we agree that the present system concentrates too much power in the hands of the police, are we not simply transferring this concentration of power to another body?

It is to avoid the concentration of too much power in police authorities — and the extreme regional variations in policing policies and methods which could ensue — that NCCL believes that the role of Parliament in relation to policing must also be considerably enhanced. Before we go on, however, to consider the role of Parliament, and other safeguards to be built into the system to limit the power of police authorities, we should note certain legal constraints which would limit the police authorities' powers from the outset.

First, the authority would only be able to instruct the police to take action that was lawful (for example, to set up a road block if they had the power, in the circumstances, to do so). Secondly, existing administrative law would limit the authorities' decisions, making it unlawful, for instance, for an authority to adopt a policy which fettered its own discretion in exercising its statutory duties. Hence it could not, for instance, adopt a policy that, say, black people should never be arrested or that the Highways Act should never be used to move travellers on. Thirdly, as we have seen, the authority could not override Parliament by instructing the police to ignore particular laws or offences altogether.

Checks and Balances

(i) Parliament

There are many policing matters which require national standards or regulations, in the interests of efficiency or uniformity or as necessary safeguards. The structure of the police force and its division into ranks are two obvious examples; there need to be basic standards for training, and rules governing the use of police equipment, such as the circumstances in which firearms may be issued and fired, and police dogs used; also rules on the use of informers and agents provocateurs, surveillance and surveillance methods, and so on.

While the Home Secretary should clearly no longer be the police authority for the Metropolitan Police he should retain certain powers over all police forces and have a duty to exercise these powers to promote the effectiveness of the police. In exercising these powers, however, his accountability to Parliament should be increased, his decisions no longer being subject only to question or negative annulment by Parliament. His areas of responsibility should be scrutinised by a permanent Select Committee of the House of Commons, which he should notify of any significant changes in policy and practices during the year. He should be required to report regularly to Parliament on the way in which he is fulfilling his responsibilities, on which MPs should, as now, be able to question him. Parliament should be required to approve positively the guidelines and standards which he sets down for the police. The Home Secretary should not retain his power to veto police authority decisions, for example their appointments or financial priorities, unless these contravene the national guidelines and standards approved by Parliament.

The Home Secretary should retain the power to order a local enquiry into the policing of an area but should be expected to publish the enquiry report. Similarly he should retain the power to require a chief constable to submit reports to him on particular issues, and an annual report.

The Home Secretary should also continue to appoint HMI Constabulary, whose authority would be extended to include the inspection of London's police force. Similarly, the Home Secretary should retain his responsibility for research into policing matters and for making regulations regarding the conditions of service and discipline. But his exercise of these powers would be open to scrutiny by the Select Committee. Consideration could be given to extending the responsibilities of the HMI beyond assessing the efficiency of each force. It could, for instance, be responsible for assessing whether each force is complying with Parliamentary guidelines and report any breaches to the Home Secretary. It could also potentially play a role in investigating instances where an authority failed in its duty to enforce the law.

(ii) Independent Prosecutor

A major objection to increasing police accountability to local politicians is the danger of corrupt influence on prosecution decisions. This will be overcome when the decision to prosecute is removed from the police and made the responsibility of a public prosecutor, accountable nationally rather than locally. NCCL has consistently argued for such a system, which already exists in Scotland; it was recommended by the Royal Commission on Criminal Procedure (RCCP) and is currently being introduced by the government in its Prosecution of Offences Bill.[10]

At present, although the Director of Public Prosecutions has sole right to instigate a prosecution in certain kinds of cases such as murder and incest, most prosecutions are brought by the police. The responsibility for deciding to bring a prosecution and for conducting the prosecution is that of the chief constable, though junior officers responsible for investigating an offence may take the decision to prosecute for a minor offence — in some forces there being policy guidelines laid down by the chief constable indicating what attitude should be taken towards prosecutions for particular offences.

The argument for removing the decision to prosecute from the police stands independently of any reforms to increase accountability to elected representatives. NCCL argued in its evidence to the RCCP[11] that it would be desirable to separate the responsibility for investigating an offence from that for bringing a prosecution because the police officers committed to investigating an offence are not detached enough to assess whether the evidence they have gathered is sufficient to prosecute. 'It offends', we argued, 'against the principle that the prosecution should be independent, impartial and fair, concerned with the truth rather than winning or losing'.

A further criticism of the present system is that the decision to prosecute should be based on public policy and individual circumstances as well as the likelihood of conviction. The police are not recruited, trained or equipped to judge these factors objectively. Above all, we argued, they are not publicly accountable for these decisions.

Finally, because the majority of prosecution decisions are taken locally, there is no uniformity of prosecution policy throughout the country so that an offence could be committed with impunity in one area but not in another. The criminal law, we argued, should outlaw behaviour on a uniform basis throughout the country so that a person will know what constitutes a crime, wherever he/she happens to be. Hence we proposed that public guidelines should be laid down by Parliament, to help prosecutors make the decision whether or not to prosecute, specifying, for example, that it was not appropriate to prosecute for a minor offence where the suspect is fatally ill or has already made restitution. Most important in the context of the reforms proposed here, the prosecution service should be accountable nationally and not to locally elected representatives, thus removing the danger of improper influence on individual prosecution decisions by a police authority.

There are many additional measures which could be introduced to enhance the accountability of the police. A Data Protection Authority with effective enforcement powers is essential to control the nature of personal information stored on police computers; statutory changes are needed to protect basic freedoms, and the police complaints procedure should be made fully independent. These points are covered by other NCCL publications.[12]

Additional Powers of the Police Authority

In order to direct their force effectively, police authorities would require specific powers. In particular we should consider the access they would require to information, the extent of their control over finance, and their role in relation to appointments, promotion, discipline, and dismissals.

(i) Access to information

One question is how much information authority members would need in order to do their job effectively and what safeguards should be included to prevent misuse of the information.

A minimum requirement is that the annual reports made by chief constables should be standardised and the provision of certain information in them made mandatory. However, it would also be necessary for members of the police authority to have access to certain police files in order to supervise effectively the use by the police of their powers and ensure that, for instance, correct procedures were being followed. Similarly, the authority would need the power to call for reports on any policing matter within their responsibility.

Much of the information which the police hold is sensitive and should only be available, whether to police officers or elected representatives, on a 'need to know' basis. The kinds of information which the police have should be categorised and Parliament should lay down in statute who should have access to which categories of information, based on their need to know. The police authority should have a duty to ensure that basic data protection principles apply, perhaps appointing a data protection officer responsible for examining the files to ensure that they contain only information which is relevant, accurate and up-to-date, and that it is only used for the policing purposes for which it was collected. In any dispute over whether the police should release information or provide a report it should be open to either party to approach the Home Secretary to arbitrate.

If authority members were to have access to sensitive information on police investigations, it might be asked, could they not use the information corruptly to undermine an investigation if friends or acquaintances of theirs were involved? The authority members would not, after all, be subject to the Police Discipline Code which forbids a police officer to disclose such information. The first safeguard should be that councillors would only have access to such information if it were necessary for them to carry out their responsibilities. Secondly, councillors who are *not* members of the authority should not have access to the information, a restriction which is supported by a recent judgement in the House of Lords.[13] Thirdly, it would be a criminal offence under the Criminal Law Act 1967 (s.4) for a member of the authority to do anything which would impede the arrest or prosecution of someone whom he or she knows or believes has committed an arrestable offence and it would similarly be an offence for him/her to take any action to 'pervert the course of justice'. Fourthly, as with other local government committees, the authority would adopt standing orders which precluded the release of confidential information and any member of the authority releasing such information would be subject to the discipline of the committee. Finally, members would be subject to the National Code of Local Government Conduct which forbids the use of confidential information 'for the personal advantage of yourself or of anyone known to you'.

Once an independent Police Complaints Authority had been established, it would no longer be necessary for the police authority to have access to the case files on police complaints. However, while the current system under the Police and Criminal Evidence Act is maintained, the police authority should be able to examine the investigating officer's file and inform the chief constable or Police Complaints Board if it is not satisfied with the way in which the complaint has been handled.

(ii) Financial control

The current position, as we have seen, is that one half of the cost of maintaining each force is provided by the county council and the other half by central government, and we have no grounds for arguing that these sources of funding should change. Similarly we have heard no suggestion that there should be any change in the practice whereby police pay, and thus a substantial proportion of the total budget, is agreed centrally (although it is not clear that the GLC proposal accounts for this, as it suggests that the authority should retain ultimate power to decide on all expenditure).

The Home Secretary should retain his power to refuse to pay the 50 per cent from central government if the force is not efficient, but the criteria on which this decision is based should be clarifed and published. Any threat to withhold the grant should similarly be made public and should relate only to the criteria of efficiency laid down. The Home Secretary should not be empowered to purchase for a force equipment which the authority has not approved but should be able to insist on the purchase of equipment which is of the type and standard approved by Parliament in the nationally agreed guidelines.

(iii) Appointments, promotion, discipline and dismissal

As in other local government departments, the authority would have ultimate responsibility for all personnel matters. In practice, it would delegate these powers to senior officers, councillors being personally involved only for the most senior appointments.

The criticism will no doubt be made that making the police employees of the authority is a recipe for improper influence by councillors on individual officers. In reply, it can be argued that the greater public exposure of police authorities, compared to the secrecy surrounding the current personnel and discipline system, would reduce the likelihood of corruption.

The authority need not take an interest in staff matters at all levels as these would, as in other local government departments, be delegated to senior officers. Not only would such involvement be unnecessarily time-consuming for councillors, but the existing local authority staff procedural agreements would prevent their playing a significant role in promotion or discipline at most levels. Disciplinary procedures take place within each department and only finally reach the council committee on appeal.

It might also be feared that making the police employees of the police authority would undermine, in a detrimental way, the hierarchical command structure of the force. If the committee could instruct junior officers, would not the authority of senior officers be undermined? In practice, of course, the committee would give instructions to the force through its senior officers, in the same way that instructions from the housing committee, for example, are conveyed through the Director of Housing. Moreover, instructions could come only from meetings of the authority. Individual councillors would not be able to issue instructions to the police, unless that authority were delegated to them by the committee, a practice which should be restricted to uncontroversial decisions and those in line with existing authority policy.

Police officers' rights as employees should be protected by their having trade union rights, including being covered by the Employment Protection Act, which would enable them, for instance, to challenge any decision to dismiss them unfairly.

Structure and Membership of Police Authorities

(i) Structure

Outside London there are currently two kinds of authority: those responsible for a force covering one county, and ten joint authorities where the force covers two or more counties.

As joint authorities cover very large areas and are not part of an existing unit of local government, it is difficult for the public to relate to the authority as a body representing their interests. Consideration must therefore be given to changing the structure of the authority and the force for which it is responsible, so that they are more accessible to the public and more readily accountable to it, while ensuring that such changes do not impair the efficiency of the force. If it does not prove practicable to divide the force so that force boundaries do coincide with those of the counties, consideration could be given to establishing a two-tier structure; a first tier representing the two or more counties and a second tier at county level. Members of the public could thus relate to the county level police committee, which would determine police priorities and methods for its area. Where the force covers only one county, the police authority should be the county council, or a committee of the council, for that area.

The government's proposal to abolish the metropolitan county councils and hence their police authorities would remove the democratic structure on which our proposals could be based in those areas. The joint boards which will exercise the existing responsibilities of police authorities, two thirds of whose members will be nominated by the district councils and one third remain non-elected magistrates, are unsuitable to exercise the powers which a police authority should have.[14] Until it is clear precisely what structure of local government will replace the councils in these areas, including London, we cannot make very specific proposals regarding the structure of their police authorities. It would be preferable for all the metropolitan areas to have a uniform structure, possibly a two-tier police authority as the GLC has proposed for London.

In London it is clearly desirable that the Home Secretary alone should no longer be the police authority and that he should be replaced by a committee of locally elected representatives representing the interests of Londoners. The structure of the authority is problematic, however, not only because of the proposed abolition of the GLC but because the Metropolitan Police is three times larger than any provincial force and covers an area slightly larger than that of the thirty-two London boroughs. Secondly, the Metropolitan Police includes within its remit certain 'national functions' such as the protection of royalty and support services such as co-ordinating mutual aid. Thirdly, London also has within it the small City of London force, separately 'accountable' to the Common Council of the City of London, an archaic institution comprised in part of aldermen elected for life.

The GLC's proposals for London were published before the government's White Paper advocating the abolition of the GLC and necessarily have to be considered in that context.

The GLC recommended that a two-tier authority be established, based on the existing local government structure, that the Metropolitan Police boundaries should be made coterminous with those of the GLC, and that the police district boundaries should match those of London boroughs. It also suggested that the City of London force be amalgamated with the Met. NCCL endorsed these proposals.

A more significant structural problem is the future of the Metropolitan Police's national functions which, it can be argued, should neither be paid for solely by Londoners nor controlled by them. The GLC divides the national functions into two categories: those related to specific institutions (e.g. protection of the monarchy) and Scotland Yard's support services (e.g. central record-keeping). In fact, it is more helpful to divide them into *operational policing* (e.g. protecting monarch, criminal investigations, Special Branch) and non-operational support services (including record-keeping, and the police laboratory).

The GLC proposed removing *all* the national police functions from the Metropolitan Police and giving them to a separate National Police Agency which would be accountable to a committee comprised of representatives from all police authorities.

NCCL questioned this proposal for two reasons: the danger, which the GLC recognises, of creating an incipient national police force; and the fact that a committee consisting of representatives from all over the country is not a practical proposition. There is no comparable national body with responsibility for a major department, and its members, with their own local government responsibilities, would not be able to meet more than once, say, every three months. They could not have the time to sit on the plethora of subcommittees which would be necessary to supervise closely the many different national functions.

The danger of creating an incipient national police force can, however, be overcome by dividing up the national functions. The GLC gives no reason why operational functions such as protecting the monarch and diplomatic personnel should remain national functions; surely the Metropolitan Police should handle these where they relate to their area in the same way that other forces deal with specialist policing problems, at ports and airports, for example? The London-wide policing squads would (as the GLC suggests) be part of the Metropolitan Police and accountable to the GLC level of the police authority, leaving only the *non-operational* national policing support services.

As there should be national guidelines/standards for these services, it seems reasonable that they should come under the Home Office but be scrutinised by the permanent Select Committee of Parliament, an option the GLC rejects because 'it would not be in a position to act as employer of the police force' — an objection which would no longer apply.

London clearly has more national policing responsibilities than any other force, and London's police should therefore continue to receive a financial subsidy from Parliament to cover the cost of their services.

The GLC Police Committee argues that the size and complexity of the Metropolitan Police requires both London-wide *and* borough-level systems of control. It also proposes that the committees at GLC and borough level should be part of the existing local government structure rather than a directly elected authority. Apart from the extra cost that such a separate bureaucracy would entail, the elected representatives would lack the experience of other local government services, such as planning and housing, which have implications for policing. It then asks: which decisions should be made at GLC level and which by the boroughs?

The GLC Police Committee believes that maximum power should be given to the borough police committees, a proposal which, it argues, would entail a radical reorganisation of the Metropolitan Police to decentralise its management structure. This is because the borough committees would have control over policing policy and priorities for their area, and work with their commander to implement these, rather than through the Met. HQ at Scotland Yard. The London-wide committee would, it is suggested, formulate detailed policies for the borough police committees to adopt, but these would be guidelines only, to be amended in the light of local views and circumstances.

The London-wide committee would determine the police precept after consultation with the boroughs and allocate the money between the districts. The borough committees would then decide how the money was spent. The London-wide committee would control the London regional police squads and carry out London-wide administrative functions, including acting as the formal employer of the staff, although the staff would be supervised by the borough committees. For those policing tasks where more than one borough is concerned, or when mutual aid is required by another borough or force, borough police committees would have a duty to provide the necessary officers to assist.

The advantage of this partnership in which control over local policing is devolved to borough police committees is, as the GLC suggests, that the policies could reflect the particular problems and needs of the vastly differing areas which exist within London's boundaries. General policies devised at London level could not reflect these differences, nor would Londoners relate so strongly to a central committee as they can to their own town hall. As the GLC Police Committee argues, giving the London-wide committee control over policing policies 'could result in creating the impression that the Metropolitan Police was under democratic control without effecting any major changes on the ground'.[15]

The GLC Police Committee rightly envisages that the London-wide committee would delegate extensive powers to the Commissioner, which might be likely to include drawing up policy guidelines and detailed regulations for the guidance of the borough police committees, responsibility for ensuring that statutes and Home Office standards of efficiency are incorporated into guidelines, and responsibility for the discipline of the force.

(ii) Membership

The members of the authorities must represent the interests of the public and be accountable to them: non-elected magistrates must therefore be removed from the authorities as they fulfil neither of these criteria. The magistrates are able to, and do, undermine democratic government by voting with opposition parties to defeat the majority, and are accountable to no one for their actions. Moreover, members of the judiciary should be seen to be independent of the police, and their presence on police authorities tarnishes their neutrality.

There would be some advantage in making the whole county council the police authority. All councillors could thus ensure that the needs of their particular area were represented and could obtain necessary information from the police, rather than having to request information via authority members when they reported back to meetings of the full council. Such an arrangement would also ensure that those familiar with all areas of council policy which affect policing, such as planning and housing, were involved in preparing policing policies and could take back the necessary lessons to their own committees. If the statutory duty to enforce the law were transferred to the authority it would properly be shared among all the councillors, who are responsible for setting the rates, and would allocate to policing the share they deemed appropriate. The obverse of this proposal is that local councillors are already overburdened and it may therefore be unrealistic to expect all councillors to attend the meetings.

Under the Local Government Act 1972[16] up to one third of a council committee can be co-opted or elected directly from the community. Recognising that the membership of many local councils (often predominantly white, male and middle-class) does not reflect the composition of the local communities they represent, there is a case for enabling representatives of minority or interest groups with particular policing needs to be co-opted, or directly elected, on to the authority to redress this imbalance.

There are arguments against this, however. If direct elections were organised, we could expect that they would still be dominated by the traditional political parties which already have support in the communities and an experienced political machine. If individuals were co-opted instead, who would decide *which* groups should be represented and whether an organisation's claim to represent a particular group is legitimate. If the co-optees were not allowed to vote, would they not rightly feel that they were being consulted and then ignored? But if they could vote, to whom would they be accountable for their actions? Could the authority insist that they report back regularly to the bodies they represent, or would this be an unacceptable interference in the internal affairs of independent organisations?

Drawing representatives directly from community groups on to the authority could, however, help to overcome one problem we have identified in the current system: the lack of accountability of those elected representatives now responsible for the police to the public. Representatives of groups experiencing particular policing problems or with particular needs would ensure that the authority was fully aware of the community's views and that this awareness was translated into action. The question of co-option is thus one which requires considerable debate before it is resolved, and one we leave open.

The GLC suggests that the London-wide committee should consist solely of GLC councillors *if*, as it recommends, the greatest degree of power is decentralised to the boroughs. If, on the other hand, the GLC committee was to be given ultimate control, its police committee should include borough representatives. Non-councillors, it argues, could have a valuable part to play on the GLC subcommittees covering particular aspects of policing (e.g. training, finance, etc.). It also recommends that the London-wide committee should *not* comprise all ninety-two GLC members but be an ordinary committee of the GLC with a larger than usual number of members.

Similarly, the GLC Police Committee suggests that the authority at borough level should be an ordinary committee of the local authority on which GLC councillors should have *ex officio* places to ensure a link with the London-wide committee. The committee should also be free to co-opt members from representatives of the community, as other council committees do now. It could also set up subcommittees, perhaps relating to particular police stations, which would provide greater opportunities for co-option of community representatives.[17]

If the GLC and metropolitan councils are abolished the kind of structure which the GLC has proposed will need to be considered in the light of the new arrangements. If there were no local government body covering the area of the police force, a directly elected police authority for that area might be necessary in each of these areas. The primary concern must be that it is a locally elected body accountable to the people whom the police are expected to serve.

Meetings of the authorities should be advertised and open to the public (except when genuinely confidential matters are being discussed such as the position of an individual officer or member of the public) and the minutes available for inspection. In order to help the authorities to be fully aware of the public's views, consultative arrangements might be desirable: holding public meetings on the policing of the area and establishing consultative committees representing local organisations and, for example, MPs for the area are two possibilities.

Conclusion

A radical transformation of the constitutional position of the police is required to place them firmly under the direction of our democratically elected representatives at local and national level. A new tripartite structure of control and accountability should be introduced which balances the powers of new local police authorities, Parliament and the police. Police authorities should have the ultimate authority to direct police policies, priorities and operations within the law, so that the elected representatives effectively determine the nature of policing in their areas, within a framework of legislation, minimum standards and guidelines established by Parliament.

Earlier proposals for reform were influenced by the belief that the police must remain independent of outside direction in order to be 'impartial' and rested on an untenable distinction between policy and operational decisions. By ensuring that the police retained control over 'operational decisions' they failed to make the police accountable for these decisions and would have enabled them to override the authority's decisions simply by claiming that an issue was an operational matter. Nor would it be feasible to give chief constables control over operational matters but to make them accountable to the authority afterwards. Neither the authority nor the chief constable would ever be clear which decisions fell within their authority.

If the authority is given the power to direct policy and operational decisions, it should have a statutory duty to enforce the law. A key question then remains whether the police should retain their statutory duty to enforce the law or whether this duty should simply be delegated to them by the authority. If the police retain this duty it would impose certain restrictions on police authorities: whether these are seen as a desirable safeguard or an unwarranted limitation of the powers of elected representatives depends on the extent to which it is thought powers should be concentrated in one body. Imposing this statutory duty on the authority *and* the police may be the most satisfactory position. It is one of many questions which will require extensive public debate before it is resolved.

Criticisms and doubts about the direction of the police by elected representatives can be answered. The anxiety that such a system puts the police under 'political control' rests on the mistaken belief that the present controllers of the police, senior police officers, are above holding their own values and prejudices, above making political decisions. The question, we argue, is whether the police should remain under the political control of a small group of senior officers (and Home Office officials) or be placed under the democratic ('political') control of elected representatives.

We have shown that the proposed system would not enable police authorities to override Parliament. Nor would it be impractical because the authorities' powers would largely be delegated, as in other public services, to chief police officers. The authorities could not give unlawful instructions nor take decisions which limited their own discretion. If they held the duty to enforce the law and failed to do so, their failure to act could be challenged in court.

To balance the authorities' powers, we believe that the responsibilities of Parliament in relation to policing must also be considerably enhanced. By issuing national guidelines Parliament would ensure minimum standards and, where necessary, uniformity of practice throughout the country. The Home Secretary, responsible for devising these guidelines, would not only be accountable to Parliament but have the exercise of his responsibilities scrutinised by an all-party Select Committee.

Additional safeguards would be provided by the establishment of an independent prosecutor system (removing the decision to prosecute both from the police and from any possible interference by the police authority); the establishment of a Data Protection Authority; and the introduction of employment protection for police officers.

Police authorities would need greater access to information about their force but only on a 'need to know' basis. Councillors would be constrained by the law and local government codes of practice from disclosing confidential information.

Chief constables should be required to produce an annual report including certain basic information, and police authorities would have the power to request a report on any police matter. In the event of a disagreement between the chief constable (or commander) and the police authority about access to information, the Home Secretary should have the power to arbitrate.

The authorities should have ultimate responsibility for appointments, promotion, discipline, and dismissal of officers, but delegate these powers in the case of most staff, as in other local government departments. It should negotiate procedural agreements which protect their staff's employment rights. Police officers should have the right to join a trade union.

The authority should continue to determine the funding required for its force, subject to predetermined requirements that are agreed nationally, and central government should continue to pay half the agreed cost.

Magistrates should be removed from provincial police authorities, which should comprise councillors of the county council covering the force area. In the ten areas where the force covers more than one county, consideration should be given to dividing the force so that its boundaries are coterminous with those of the county. Alternatively, the joint authorities, which would be divided into two tiers, should consist of councillors delegated by each county council to represent them. Consideration must also be given to whether it would be desirable for police authorities to accept co-opted representatives of local groups.

The proposed abolition of the metropolitan councils, including the GLC, would remove the local government structure on which our proposals could be based. We cannot make specific recommendations on the form which the authorities should take in these areas until the present uncertain situation has been resolved. The primary consideration must be that the authority should comprise locally elected representatives accountable to the public. It is clearly desirable that the role of the Home Secretary as sole police authority in London be replaced by a locally elected committee with the same structure as in the metropolitan areas outside London and the same powers as all police authorities in England and Wales.

The Metropolitan Police and City of London forces should be amalgamated and the boundaries of the Metropolitan Police and its districts made coterminous with those of the London-wide elected body and the London boroughs. The Metropolitan Police's national functions should be divided up, the operational responsibilities remaining those of the Metropolitan Police (which should receive a financial subsidy reflecting the disproportionate national responsibilities fulfilled by them) while the non-operational support services should come under the Home Office, scrutinised by a Select Committee of Parliament.

The authorities would delegate day-to-day responsibility for the direction of their forces, according to their policies, to senior officers. It has to be expected that the police and community representatives would work together co-operatively in the interests of the communities they serve. The defensive, secretive stance which the police often adopt now when faced with criticism would be unnecessary if the police authority had greater responsibility for their actions and perhaps a greater understanding of the problems which the police themselves face than is possible under the present system.

One final problem remains, and this we address in the next chapter: having identified the outline of a new system of accountability which we believe is desirable and workable, how do we bring it about?

Notes

1. Mr. Whitelaw on *Weekend World*, 15 November 1981.
2. 'A Report on Relationships between the Police and the Public in South Yorkshire' (South Yorkshire County Council, 1979).
3. *The Guardian*, 14 January 1981.
4. Jack Straw MP, 'Memorandum on the Police Authorities Powers Bill' (November 1979).
5. Minutes of the meeting of Greater Manchester Police Committee held on 5 June 1981.
6. 'A New Police Authority for London: A Consultation Paper on Democratic Control of the Police in London', GLC Police Committee Discussion Paper No.1 (GLC, March 1983).
7. *Ibid.*, para.156.
8. *Ibid.*, para.139.
9. *Ibid.*, para.155.
10. *Report of the Royal Commission on Criminal Procedure* (1981), Cmnd 8092.
11. Submission of the NCCL to the Royal Commission on Criminal Procedure, Part 1. A Public Prosecutor (1979).
12. E.g. Patricia Hewitt, *A Fair Cop* (NCCL, 1982); NCCL Briefing 'Data Protection Bill' (1983).
13. *City of Birmingham District Council* v. *O* [1983] 1 All ER 497.

14. *Streamlining the Cities,* Government Proposals for Reorganising Local Government in Greater London and the Metropolitan Counties (October 1983), White Paper, Cmnd 9063. Nominations from the district councils will, the White Paper states, 'reflect *as closely as practicable* the balance of parties on the *nominating* authority. This will in general have practical effect only where an authority is making nominations *for more than two seats* for a joint board' (our emphasis). Yet the White Paper suggests that a high proportion of councils will have only two nominations and the vast majority only two or three. The political composition of the joint boards, even excluding the non-elected magistrates, will therefore bear little relation to the actual balance of parties in the district councils or in the area as a whole.
15. 'A New Police Authority for London', *op.cit.,* , para.211.
16. S.102 (3)
17. 'A New Police Authority for London', *op.cit.*, paras.215-22.

CHAPTER 6
Campaigning for Democratic Control of the Police

Only Parliament can change the law to bring the police under democratic control. The present Conservative government has stated that it will not do this.[1] Its Police and Criminal Evidence Act fails to increase the powers of police authorities or to establish a locally elected police authority for London.

The Labour Party, however, is committed by its 1983 Annual Conference to 'the creation of democratically elected police authorities in all parts of the country including London, with statutory responsibilities for policy and operational control of the police and recruitment and training practices'.

One year previously, at its 1982 Assembly, the Liberal Party had similarly called for 'decentralised control of the police authorities, including the Metropolitan Police, with elected representatives having the power to decide on budget, policy, operational strategy and the employment of senior officers'. Further, the police should also have a statutory duty to consult with local authorities and other local bodies.

In contrast, the Social Democratic Party, in a policy document published in 1983, argued that

> . . . reforms are needed to enable police authorities to be more effective in using their existing powers. Much clearer guidance should be given to police authorities on matters on which they should take an active concern. Police authorities, too, should not be wholly made up of councillors and magistrates, but should more widely represent the variety of interests in the community, including voluntary and neighbourhood organisations.

In relation to the Metropolitan Police the document argues that

The demands made on the police in London set them apart from other constabularies. Their responsibilities for royalty, Parliament, the diplomatic corps and other national and international institutions, together with the increased scope and scale of demonstrations held in the capital, justifies the continuance of the Home Secretary as police authority for London.[2]

During the House of Commons committee stage of the Police and Criminal Evidence Bill, the Labour opposition attempted (unsuccessfully) to insert amendments into the Bill to put each force 'under the direction of the police authority', which would have a duty to 'prepare and publish a policy for its area which lays down the policing priorities to be adopted and the proposed allocation of resources'.

The sole Liberal MP on the committee, Alex Carlile, moved (also unsuccessfully) an amendment which sought to create a police authority for London comprised of locally elected and nominated members 'responsible for the policing of the Metropolitan Police District' which would have the power to 'determine, from time to time, the general policy and operational strategy of the Metropolitan Police'. The Metropolitan Commissioner could, however, object to or defer discussion by the authority of a particular operation if he considered that it would seriously prejudice the success of the operation, the Home Secretary being the arbiter in any dispute.

Party conference decisions are not necessarily included in the party's election manifesto. Still less do they ensure that the policy will actually be implemented if the party later forms the government. The resolve of those parties committed to some form of accountability therefore needs to be strengthened if their relatively new commitments are eventually to be implemented. But there are also many other forms which the campaign for democratic control of the police is taking, and could take in the future. We mention here just a few of them.

Encouraging Police Authorities to Use Their Existing Powers

Some authorities are, as we have seen, now making use of their statutory powers to influence the policies and practices of their force and to encourage it to be responsive to local needs. (Significantly it is some of these authorities which will cease to exist if the government's proposals to abolish the metropolitan authorities are enacted.) Most authorities have not adopted such a positive approach, however, and there is considerable scope for local groups and councillors to encourage them to do so. The aim of such a campaign would be threefold:

(i) To ensure that local people are exerting some influence over the policing of their area now, using the police authority's existing, albeit limited, powers.
(ii) To draw attention to the limitations of those powers, where an authority is unsuccessful in bringing about a desired change in force policy or methods, and to increase awareness of the need for a change in the law to increase the authority's, and Parliament's, powers.
(iii) To highlight, in some areas, the reluctance of authority members to exercise their powers, if, for example, members refuse to call for a report on a local policing issue of concern; or to draw attention to the undemocratic nature of these committees, if the non-elected magistrates unite with a minority party to out-vote the elected majority.

An example of a local group encouraging its local police authority to respond to local needs when exercising its existing powers is provided by NCCL's Northumberland and Durham group. When the group learnt that the Durham Police Authority was about to appoint a new chief constable in 1981, it wrote to each member of the authority suggesting what qualities they should look for in the candidates.

The group originally addressed the letter only to the chairman of the authority, but he refused to circulate it to the committee members, saying: 'I do not believe that the view of any one group should influence the judgement of the Committee in relation to an appointment'. The group's response was to circulate the letter to authority members itself.

The letter argued that, because the authority could not direct the chief constable as it could other chief officers, it was vital that authority members select someone who shared their views as to how County Durham should be policed and who would heed the advice they gave him. Among the questions the group advised the committee to consider were the candidates' attitudes to reactive and community policing methods, police-community relations, suspects' rights in detention, domestic violence, and bans on marches.[3]

There are many other ways in which police authorities can be encouraged to use their existing powers. Arising out of their supervisory role in relation to police complaints, for example, the authority could examine the pattern of complaints and discuss with the chief constable the kind of policing methods which give rise to most complaints, such as the exercise of stop-and-search powers.

Arising out of their control over the budget, the authority should ask: is our force good value for money? Members can seek an explanation for the chosen distribution of resources and can decide, for example, whether money should be allocated to a new sub-station, to a supply of plastic bullets, or to the purchase of Transit vans.

The authority's responsibility for the efficiency of its force should lead it to ask whether task forces, such as special patrol groups, are efficient; it could call for a report from the chief constable on the effect on crime of an SPG operation — to include information about the surrounding areas where, it has been suggested, street crime transfers only to return when the SPG have departed.

Public co-operation is crucial to police effectiveness, and each authority could question its chief constable about the enforcement of safeguards for suspects in detention in his police stations, such as access to a solicitor, on the grounds that abuse of these rights is a major source of public distrust and hostility. Similarly, they could ask about the clear-up rate in relation to different kinds of crime and about force policy in relation to racist attacks, domestic disputes, and many other important issues, depending on local circumstances.

If an authority is to question its chief constable effectively, it needs to be kept informed by the public, local groups and councillors not on the authority. They should not only press authority members to make use of their powers but provide them with the information they need to do so effectively. The police authority should be the forum for raising issues of local concern about policing and should be encouraged to meet frequently, and in public.

Asking police authorities to obtain information from their force is another way to encourage councillors to find out what their force is doing and, in some cases, where information is refused, to highlight an unnecessary degree of secrecy about police policies and operational decisions. Councillors who are not on the authority can take the opportunity at meetings of the full council to ask the authority's representative about the authority's exercise of its responsibilities.

The campaign cannot focus solely on police authorities' use of their existing powers, however. Where these powers prove inadequate, for example when the chief constable refuses to change his policy or even to provide information, public attention can be drawn to this through the local media. When local cases and incidents illustrate the lack of accountability you can write to the press to point this out. In addition you could write to your MP saying that you think the police should be made more accountable, and put motions calling for a campaign for a change in the law to the organisations of which you are a member.

Everyone is concerned about policing — whether it be for their right to demonstrate, their safety in the streets at night, or protection from burglaries. There is therefore plenty of scope for co-operation with other local groups in a joint campaign, which will be stronger if it represents a broad cross-section of the community. You could draw up a list of all the local groups you know of in your area — including groups campaigning on the environment, ethnic minority organisations, trade unions, groups working with the elderly, social clubs, parent-teacher associations, tenants' associations, women's groups, gay groups, youth clubs, and transport pressure groups — and consider what their particular concerns about policing might be. Discuss these with them, and where possible work together.

You could ask your local force for information about their policies and practices in relation to issues which affect you as a woman, for example, or as a trade unionist. You could make known your views on these policies and practices and organise public meetings on policing issues of current concern, always linking them to the need for accountability.

Groups could devise a questionnaire for local and parliamentary candidates to find out their views on the kind of policing needed in the area and on the need for democratic control. You could also conduct a survey in your area, perhaps concentrating on a particular group such as the elderly, to find out what they think police priorities and methods should be, and pass this information on to the authority or, in London, to your borough council.

Campaigning in London

The campaign in London has, necessarily, taken a unique form because there is no locally elected police authority. The campaign gained a new impetus in May 1981 when a Labour administration gained control of the Greater London Council pledged to 'campaign for a police authority consisting solely of members of the GLC and London boroughs to have control over the Metropolitan and City Police'.

This commitment followed initiatives by certain London boroughs, including Lewisham's threat to refuse to pay the police precept (see chapter 3) and Lambeth Council's enquiry into community-police relations in Lambeth in 1981, which resulted from a succession of controversial SPG visits to the borough and the breakdown of its ineffective police-community liaison committee. Other local bodies, for example trades councils, have initiated unofficial enquiries into particular policing practices. NCCL itself organised an unofficial enquiry into the policing of the anti-fascist demonstration in Southall on 23 April 1979 at which Blair Peach died, after the Home Secretary, as police authority, had refused to establish an official enquiry under the 1964 Police Act, and more recently into the policing of the 1984-5 miners' dispute.

The manifesto on which the Labour GLC was elected in 1981 said that it would 'monitor the work of the police force as a prelude to its gaining power to control the police'. The new administration immediately established its own 'Police Committee' to fulfil these commitments, with a Support Unit which includes lawyers and researchers.

As part of its monitoring exercise, it established two enquiries into vandalism and racial harassment, to which local groups gave evidence, and publishes a regular free newsletter, *Policing London*. Its direct response to Metropolitan Police practices has been critical. It rejected the Metropolitan Police Commissioner's 1981 Annual Report as 'inadequate', opposed his replacement by Sir Kenneth Newman,[4] and called on him to make all documents dealing with policing policy publicly available, without success.

The GLC Police Committee has also attempted to influence national policing policy, opposing the Home Secretary's proposals for police consultative committees, supporting instead the establishment of borough police committees and later expressing its 'total opposition' to the Police and Criminal Evidence Bill. In 1983 it launched a public consultation exercise around its paper 'A New Police Authority for London'.[5]

The response to the GLC's initiatives from both government and police has been hostile[6] — although the London paper *The Standard*, renowned for its hostility to the GLC Labour administration, conceded that the proposals in the consultative paper did 'merit examination': 'It may be that a scheme to devolve some responsibility for local policing to local borough police authorities deserves serious attention . . . But GLC participation in such a scheme would be wrong as well as superfluous'.[7]

Independent Police Monitoring Groups

The GLC could not monitor the whole of the Metropolitan Police area alone, and its Police Committee decided to encourage the development of the local police monitoring groups which were springing up in boroughs throughout London.

The Committee has supported applications for funding from a wide variety of groups, some monitoring all aspects of the policing of their area, others focusing on particular areas of concern such as police handling of racist attacks or of 'public order' incidents, or police treatment of gay people. The Institute of Race Relations received funding to analyse press coverage of specific aspects of the relationship between the police and black people, including the presentation of black people in relation to crime, public order incidents, and the police inability/failure to give the black community protection from racial violence.[8]

The Gay London Police Monitoring Group received a small grant to enable it to produce 50,000 legal advice cards for gay people in London, while the Hillingdon Legal Resources Project received funding for two years to carry out research into the work of the police juvenile bureau in schools.

Many of the area-based groups arose out of issues of local concern, such as the police raid on a multi-racial children's party in Tower Hamlets in May 1981, which was the catalyst for the formation of the Community Alliance for Police Accountability (CAPA). While some groups, such as CAPA, have devoted considerable resources to advising people about their rights, others have devoted more time to monitoring police practices and refer individuals who need advice to other organisations. Each group has its own priorities and objectives, those of the Hayes Police Monitoring Group in Hillingdon (an outer London borough), established in June 1982, being, for example:

1. To record, collect, collate and publicise information on the activities and organisation of the Metropolitan Police in the local area, including harassment or other misconduct by police officers.
2. To promote campaigns on matters concerning local police activity, which are detrimental to the interests of members of the local community.
3. To monitor the use being made in the local area of legislation and the use of police discretion which is particularly sensitive from a civil liberties or community relations point of view, e.g. the Criminal Attempts Act.
4. To consider the organisation and operation of an emergency telephone/advice service and to co-operate with those who already provide emergency telephone/advice services.
5. To promote alternative methods of policing which would be

supported by the community and responsive to community needs.
6. To promote proper safeguards for the rights of suspects detained in custody in police stations.
7. To contribute to a London-wide campaign to promote full democratic accountability of the police to the community.
8. To encourage youth to get actively involved in the campaigning, publicity and fund-raising of the group and to maintain contact with youth by social events (gigs, discos, etc).
9. To promote these aims within the local area and to invite affiliation from all those groups and parties that share our aims
10. The group shall promote and support groups in the locality which form themselves in specific geographic or interested areas related to Police Monitoring and the General Meeting may delegate any of its responsibilities to such groups.[9]

CAPA's 24-hour emergency helpline, staffed by volunteers trained by lawyers, also serves as an important source of information, as do the youth clubs and schools in which it undertakes a teaching programme, informing children about their legal rights and leading discussions about policing issues.[10]

The majority of those who approach CAPA for help are black or Asian, and a common complaint is police reluctance to prosecute racist attackers. CAPA was able to focus press attention on this when it helped a Bengali woman who had been attacked in August 1982 by a group of white youths armed with metal-studded clubs. The police refused to take action against her attackers and failed initially even to take a written statement from her. With CAPA's assistance, the victim took out a private prosecution and two youths were convicted of her assault in January 1983.

Many of the monitoring groups have been critical of the police-community liaison committees which exist in their areas and have concluded that 'Accountability, not consultation, is the aim'. Wandsworth Policing Campaign, for example, pressed its local council and community groups to refuse to participate in the proposed post-Scarman liaison committee in Wandsworth until certain conditions were met. It wanted recognition that 'such liaison is only a first stage towards the full operational control of the police by local people', and agreement that police representatives should be prepared to discuss fully any item on the agenda (agreed in advance between local groups and the police) and provide any relevant information (unless it is *sub judice*). Finally, it insisted that 'the police should take account of, and act upon, the decisions of such meetings'.

Other monitoring group activities have included organising a call-out system to ensure observers are present at incidents involving the police; organising opposition to the Police and Criminal Evidence Bill; holding public meetings and organising press coverage of local incidents and cases, and organising a system of contact points throughout their area, at the offices of different religious, ethnic and political groups, to which individuals could report policing incidents, to be collated centrally by the monitoring group.

London Boroughs

In May 1982 the GLC's campaign for statutory powers to control London's police was backed up by the election of a number of Labour-controlled borough councils with a similar manifesto commitment. By mid-1983 nine Labour boroughs had set up police committees or subcommittees, while the remaining four were involved in consultative arrangements.[11]

The manifesto on which Hackney's council had been elected cited six particular areas of concern: the poor crime clear-up rate; inadequate policing of council estates; complaints from members of the ethnic minority communities about the behaviour of officers, including racist abuse and under- and over-reaction to incidents involving black people; the failure to protect women from violence; the policing of industrial and political disputes; and the treatment of suspects in police custody. It asserted: 'until the police are more democratically accountable to the local community as a whole, and are seen to be tackling the problems we have outlined, the support and confidence of the whole community, so necessary for effective policing, will never be achieved'.

At its first meeting on 28 July, Hackney Police Committee identified its role as 'an interim measure, the best structure obtainable at the present time, until a statutory police authority for London comprised of elected representatives of the people is established'. It agreed that it would pursue the following principle aims:

- Developing effective ways of determining the kind of policing the people of Hackney want and promoting public discussion.
- Monitoring police activity where disquiet is expressed, receiving complaints, investigating, reporting where appropriate.
- Helping the victims of crime by strengthening or establishing victim support schemes.
- Examining wider questions of police training, deployment, methods of working and institutional racism.

- Campaigning by example for police accountability.
- Drawing on the GLC Police Committee's experience and resources and contributing a Hackney dimension to their work.
- Promoting public education on such matters as legal rights, redress of grievances, crime prevention, etc.
- Developing practices where an independent element at police stations can check observance of Judges' Rules on the treatment of suspects, in anticipation of controversial incidents, troubleshooting when these occur.
- Ensuring that, where formal council-police contact takes place, it is constructive and conducted with the borough's people as the first consideration.
- Building up relations with voluntary and community organisations to work towards the establishment of an independent police monitoring group in Hackney.

The subsequent involvement of Hackney Council in the controversy surrounding the death of Colin Roach at Stoke Newington police station, and its dispute with its local force and the Home Office over a consultative committee, are described in chapter 3. Other issues in which Hackney and the other police committees have been involved include crime prevention, victim support schemes, prostitution, multi-agency co-operation, including the incorporation of a crime prevention dimension into the work of other council committees, abandoned vehicles, play facilities and their effect on the crime rate, the special patrol group, the police property-marking scheme, and the monitoring of police complaints.[12]

Of the nineteen non-Labour boroughs none has established a police committee, the majority having set up, or being in the process of setting up, consultative committees.

Conclusion

None of these initiatives will bring the police under effective democratic control. They will not make the police genuinely accountable to the public for their actions.

This can only be brought about by a change in the law to establish a radically different structure of accountability along the lines suggested in the previous chapter. But these initiatives are needed to build up the momentum for that change — and to try to ensure that the police are more sensitive now to the needs and priorities of the communities they are appointed to serve.

The momentum for change has indeed increased dramatically

over the past few years, but it is only when the campaign is successful in achieving legislative reform that we shall finally have the machinery of accountability that will enable the public to determine how each force should meet the policing needs of the whole community.

Notes

1. E.g. *Hansard*, 5 February 1981, written answer, col.166.
2. SDP Council for Social Democracy, *Urban Policy*, Policy Document No.9 (undated).
3. Internal NCCL correspondence; *Darlington and Stockton Times*, 26 September 1981; *The Journal*, 23 September 1981; *Evening Dispatch*, 24 September 1981.
4. *The Guardian*, 26 March 1982.
5. 'A New Police Authority for London: A Consultation Paper on Democratic Control of the Police in London', GLC Police Committee Discussion Paper No.1 (GLC, March 1983).
6. E.g., *The Guardian*, 1 April 1982; *The Standard*, 22 November 1982.
7. *The Standard*, 6 January 1983.
8. GLC Police Committee, document PC 6720.82.
9. Hayes Police Monitoring Group, internal papers.
10. See, for example, CAPA Annual Report, 1982.
11. *Policing London* 7 (April/May 1983).
12. Minutes of the meetings of the police committees; see also *Hackney Gazette*, 6 April 1984.

Other titles on policing and criminal procedure available from NCCL

Controlling the Constable £7.95
Tony Jefferson and *Roger Grimshaw*. The question of how far police should be accountable for their actions has become extremely vexed. The authors examine constabulary independence and the relevant legal history, and on this basis re-assess Brixton prior to the 1981 Disturbances and Southall on 23 April 1979. They conclude that a new approach to the conflict between legal authority and democratic authority is urgently needed.
Frederick Muller/Cobden Trust 1984.
ISBN 0 584 11088 X
224 pages 216 × 138 mm

Poor Law: the mass arrests of homeless claimants in Oxford £1.95
Ros Franey. The mass arrest of homeless claimants in Oxford was front page news, after the so-called 'sting'. Serious breaches of civil liberties occurred in the way in which the courts and the police treated both those charged with offences and the 100 released without charge. A unique and thorough investigation of what really happened that day, and subsequently.
NCCL, CHAR, CPAG, Claimants Defence Committee and National Association of Probation Officers 1983.
ISBN 0 906951 04 6.

A Fair Cop: Reforming the Police Complaints Procedure £1.75
Patricia Hewitt. NCCL has long argued that the only way in which the police complaints procedure could become fully effective would be to introduce an independent investigative element. This would both increase public confidence in the police and protect the rights of police officers as employees. This book looks at the history of the complaints procedure (hardly changed at all this century) and proposes the major reforms necessary.
NCCL 1982. ISBN 0 946088 01 2.

Civil Disorder and Civil Liberties: Evidence to the Scarman Enquiry £1.00
NCCL's evidence to the Scarman Enquiry argues that repressive measures are no solution to civil disorder. A positive choice must be made 'to tackle the political, economic and social divisions from which the violence has sprung and, particularly, to deal with the policing methods and attitudes that have made the police the targets of the violence'.
NCCL 1981. ISBN 0 901108 96 0.

Civil Liberties and the Miners' Dispute £1.50
NCCL Inquiry Panel. NCCL established the only independent national inquiry into the civil liberties implications of policing and the administration of justice in the miners' dispute. This interim report has provoked a wide ranging debate about the implications of the policing of the strike.
NCCL 1984. ISBN 0 946088 11 X. 40 pages

Policing the Miners' Strike £4.95
Edited by Bob Fine and *Robert Millar.* This book brings together a series of essays which analyse the significance of the developments in policing and the administration of justice during the miners' dispute.
Lawrence & Wishart/Cobden Trust 1985. 256 pages

Political Policing in Wales £1.50
Dr John Davies, Lord Gifford QC and *Tony Richards.* This is the official report of a unique public inquiry held in South Wales into policing and the investigation of politically motivated offences in Wales. It considers the implications of this, and makes recommendations for more accountable and legitimate forms of policing.
Welsh Campaign for Civil and Political Liberties 1984. ISBN 0 947740 00 7. 112 pages

Operation Fire/Operation Tan £1.25
Selwyn Jones, Penny Smith and *Philip Thomas.* Bilingual text detailing police operations in Wales investigating arson in holiday cottages.
Welsh Campaign for Civil and Political Liberties 1980.

Southall: 23 April 1979 £2.20
The report of the unofficial committee of enquiry.
NCCL 1980. ISBN 0 901108 85 5.

The Death of Blair Peach £1.50
The supplementary report deals with the day's single most disastrous event.
NCCL 1980. ISBN 0 901108 91 X.

Submissions to the Royal Commission on Criminal Procedure £3.00 complete
NCCL's submission to the Commission which will have a profound effect on Law and Order in the 1980s: A public prosecutor, 50p; Arrest, 50p; Search, seizure and surveillance, 50p; The interrogation process, 50p; Bail, photographing and fingerprinting, 50p; Police complaints, 'Sus', 50p; Identification, 50p; Preparation for trial, 25p.
NCCL 1979

Plus postage and packing @ 25p for orders up to £1.95, 40p for orders between £2.00 and £4.95, 75p for orders between £5.00 and £9.95, above £10 — post free.

NCCL, 21 Tabard Street, London SE1 4LA